D1030919

THE EDWARDIAN LADY

The Author

THE EDWARDIAN LADY

by

SUSAN TWEEDSMUIR

GERALD DUCKWORTH & CO. LTD.
3 HENRIETTA STREET, LONDON, W.C.2

First published 1966
©*1966 by* SUSAN LADY TWEEDSMUIR

Printed in Great Britain by
The Camelot Press Ltd., London and Southampton

TO

ALICE

"Well, the Edwardians, like the Elizabethans, the Jacobeans, the Carolines, the Georgians, the Victorians, were a mixed lot. This attempt to class them, to stigmatise them with adjectives, is unscientific, sentimental, and wildly incorrect. But, because it is rather more interesting than to admit frankly that they were merely a set of individuals, it will always be done."

Told by an Idiot, ROSE MACAULAY

CONTENTS

LIST OF ILLUSTRATIONS

Plates V, VI, X, XII, and XIV by courtesy of Paul Popper

WHEN it was suggested to me that I should write this book I felt that anything I could write in the way of a book about Edwardian days was only adding one more to the many works which have come out in recent years—in fact would be superfluous.

However, it was argued that many of those books have been written by men and women who did not themselves live through these years, and who write about them merely as history.

While I admire the intelligence of these writers and the painstaking research they have put into collecting and assembling facts about the Edwardian era, it often seems to me that they have got some things about the years before the First World War a little wrong, and a little false to the truth, because it is not recollected at first hand. So I will try to write down something of what I remember personally, and, if I can, recapture the atmosphere of the time I lived through in my youth.

I am sitting in my room at the falling close of a winter's day with the sky outside my window turning a faint rose colour, which puts me into the right mood for recollecting the past.

My father was Norman Grosvenor, the third son of Lord Robert Grosvenor who later was created Lord Ebury (Ebury Street in London is called after him). My mother was Caroline Stuart Wortley, daughter of James Stuart Wortley, who as Recorder of London was struck by a partial paralysis when he might have become Speaker of the House of Commons.

The Stuart Wortleys and Grosvenors had a long record as landowners of large estates in Cheshire, London and Yorkshire. My Ebury grandparents lived in a majestic Palladian house, Moor Park in Hertfordshire, where I spent a great deal of my childhood. This was home to all my cousins and myself, with its undulating park, and its secret and charming Pleasure Ground.

The Pleasure Ground has now been cut up and houses built in it, so it lives only in a few elderly hearts. If only one had the power to evoke its image and make it live in words—greenness, green trees, green shade, and golden sunshine on the water. Just for a few weeks each year the rhododendrons were mirrored in the pond. In early spring there was the astonishment of five camelia trees growing in a sort of alcove in the wood—pyramids of colour. There was a fiery splash of azaleas in their season, but mostly it was green, which made the colour when it was there, dramatic—like an explosion seen from afar.

When not at Moor Park, we lived in London. Our house in Green Street, Mayfair, was charming, with a small garden in which one large plane tree grew and flourished, and so was our subsequent Upper Grosvenor Street house with its pretty curving staircase and large drawing-rooms; it was pulled down to make room for the present Grosvenor House Hotel.

My mother loved the months during which she lived in London in her own house. She was devoted to her husband's family, but she found the give and take of a family life at Moor Park trying, and her boredom at having no household of her own to look after filled her with a sense of frustration. She painted spirited and ambitious water colours, and kept herself busy in the country.

My father's niece, Maud Grosvenor (Mrs. Maurice Glyn) writes of her youth:

"Caroline and Uncle Norman lived opposite Grandmama

and Grandpapa at the head of the oak staircase and Norman had a tiny attic where he could work at his music. Sophie had no sitting-room, and we all spread, or rather crowded about in the rest of the house. Bertie and Hugh always used my bedroom as a sitting-room and it was in those days that I acquired my nocturnal habits, for they seldom went to bed before 2 a.m.

"The atmosphere was sometimes strained, though their training in selflessness and *bienséance ordinaire* kept the surface smooth. I wonder how they all managed it. Such strong individualities thrown together! Auntie Siss, Auntie B., my mother, Caroline, Norman, Sophie, Algy, Dick and finally Queenie. I think a common dislike of my mother may have been a bond among the female part of the family. The Uncles were happy-go-lucky people, devoted to whatever game happened to be in season and living their own lives serenely. It must have been awful for Caroline with no home of her own, and Uncle Norman hidden in his attic absorbed in his music—though his great charm and lovableness must have made up for many things. When at long last my grandfather died they were all on amiable terms, and that is an achievement one must have witnessed to appreciate."

When my grandfather died we lived entirely in London and after my father's death we went less and less to Moor Park. My mother went on living at 30 Upper Grosvenor Street, in a house very large by modern standards. She let it to strangers who always seemed willing to take it on short leases. One lady said, I remember, that she liked the dining-room, as she frequently had over thirty people to dinner, all at little tables. She felt that our pillared dining room was ideally suited to her arrangements.

My parents were both interesting people, my father a musician and composer, who worked in the Sun Life insurance office, my mother a hardworking and serious artist. My mother's family were musicians of an excellent kind, one of my uncles was a portrait painter; my father's family had only slight artistic leanings but they had shown ability in various other fields. My uncle, the second Lord Ebury, had excellent business ability and was the first chairman of the Army and Navy Stores. His fellow peers thought this odd. My father's brother, Thomas Grosvenor, was a diplomat who undertook a remarkable journey when he was posted to our Legation in Peking, by going on a mission to the Yunnan province of China, the first European to go there. He married the daughter of Mr. Wells Williams, the American Minister in Pekin, and he was considered by the Foreign Office to have the stature to become an Ambassador. But sadly enough he died one bitter winter in Saint Petersburg of pneumonia at the age of forty-six.

My father's mother, Charlotte Wellesley, niece of the Iron Duke, had brought some of the Wellesley ability and driving force into the gentler and more casual Grosvenor family. The Wellesley strain was also said to have brought with it into the Ebury family what was then called "corneriness", the power to withdraw themselves and indulge in vexation with their fellow human beings. My father showed little of this, but my mother said that if he disliked anyone whom he was sitting next to at dinner she could see it from "the set of his shoulders". This was put down, perhaps unjustly, to his Wellesley blood. He never showed anything of this to his wife or family, and he was courtesy itself to servants and poorer people.

He was considered a rebel by his relations, as he was an agnostic and a Liberal, leaning alarmingly, they thought, towards radicalism. They were extremely conventional in their outlook and although good landowners, generous and public-spirited, they wished to keep things as they were.

My father's friends they considered odd. He preferred the

society of William Morris when he was young, and later that of Burne-Jones, Arthur Myers and Edmund Gurney, to those who lived more outwardly splendid and *rangé* lives.

My mother, though she was a devoted wife, remained a silent but convinced Conservative all her life. She fiercely detested Mr. Gladstone, which was strange, because owing to her partly Scotch ancestry she held sacred the ties of relationship, and Mr. Gladstone had married her mother's first cousin, which should have ensured him some favourable consideration.

This was the background which shaped my character and outlook.

In writing of any period of time those who claim in the minutest degree to be historians (or only humble commentators on the past), must realise that the older generations persist in their mental attitudes, and that this overlapping makes no one period of time clear and well-defined.

(This was particularly true of the period after the First World War when the younger generation claimed a licence of behaviour which shocked their parents, who still thought in terms of pre-war days, and who mistakenly supposed that life in the 1920s would follow the social pattern of the years before 1914.)

I realise now how much people in Edwardian times thought that things would always go on just as they always had done. The middle-aged and the old handed out a great deal of advice to the young from their own experience, often with disastrous results, or if not disastrous, singularly useless in a world which was rapidly changing. These mature people counted on a continuity of circumstances which seems extraordinary to us now, considering that they had had plenty of wars to shake their complacency—the Franco-Prussian, the Crimean, and later the Boer War, not to mention other wars of a more remote kind. The Boer War undermined the complacency of some people and Queen Victoria's death brought an era to an end, but this was not generally apparent at the time, and the daily life of the upper and middle classes outwardly continued much as before.

This makes Edward the Seventh's reign hard to write about. It lasted only a short nine years and is regarded by some people of later generations as a golden age—an age with some relaxation of morals and some removal of taboos, combined with an affluence that enabled a great many people to live very comfortably and enjoy social life and the arts. Because of the cheapness of labour, food, and commodities of all sorts, and the very small incidence of taxation, a pleasant life was within many people's reach. Human beings always, it is said, put the golden age of life back into the past, it never exists in the present. Milton says:

> And if our joyous song
> Inwraps our fancy long
> Time will run back and fetch the age of gold.

Alas, Time has shown no signs of doing this to our war-torn and exhausted century, and so some of us are inclined to exalt the Edwardian era as our Age of Gold. If I am able to point out the advantages and drawbacks of being young at this time, it is because I lived through it, and can show where the current conceptions of so-called young ladyhood went wrong.

My father had died when he was just over fifty, and my mother, although she had a complete Pre-Raphaelite drawing room with the Morris willow-pattern wall-papers and chintzes, and de Morgan plates round the walls, had, after his death, been drawn into the more worldly and conventional orbit in which our families on both sides revolved.

The girls of my generation were supposed to marry and to marry well, *i.e.* some man with money and a country estate.

I.   The Author's Mother—Caroline Grosvenor

II.   The Author's Aunt—Margaret Talbot (1907)

They were still supposed to fill up their time with a little painting, a little reading, some music, to stay about in country houses, go to dances, and generally play a sort of waiting game until the right (or wrong) man came along. It seems incredible in the context of the 1960s, but it was so, and it had the result that some of us wasted a lot of those precious years of youth.

My mother put all her artistic ability and capacity for hard work into a memorial headstone for my father's grave. It has an austere beauty, and it is, I believe, still admired in Northwood Churchyard, where my parents lie close to the Victorian church which my grandfather built in 1854. It was a long time before, after many vicissitudes, a bronze cast finally satisfied my mother's fastidious taste. Her powers of strenuous application to her art influenced me.

She was a reader too and approved of my reading steadily; in every moment of the day when I could I slipped off to my books. I had a passion for Amiel's *Journal*,* and a love for the Swiss philosopher which was intense and consuming. His gentle pessimism delighted me. Young people, especially if they have little to do, and are not poor, are much inclined to pessimism. I used to murmur his initials H. F. A. under my breath as I walked about the house, and in a book with shiny black covers I copied out long extracts from his *Journal*!

I remember, however, one evening when I had taken but a scant interest in some family and domestic crisis, my mother saying with pardonable annoyance: "You will never be any good in life if you take no interest in what is going on round you, but sit about with a notebook and pencil making extracts from Amiel's *Journal*." No one has ever realised what Amiel meant to me. Some years ago I went to Vevey and took *Le Journal intime* with me and read

* *Fragment d'un Journal intime*, Henri Frederic Amiel.

it by the lake, and I found that the phrases which haunted my youth still charmed me, notably these two passages:

"Heure nocturne, heure de silence et de solitude, tu as de la grâce et de la méllancholie, tu attendris et tu consoles; tu nous parle de tout ce qui n'est plus, et de tout qui doît mourir mais tu nous dis: Courage, et tu nous promets le repos."

And this extract also: "La vie est bien la fleur de l'herbe qu'un matin fane et qu'un coup d'air fauche; c'est bien lu lampe de veuve qu'un filet d'air éteint. Pour sentir vivement la poésie des roses d'un matin, il faut sortir des griffes d'un vautour qu'on appelle maladie. Le font et le rehaut de tout c'est la cimetière. La seule certitude en ce monde d'agitations vaines, et d'inquiétudes infinies, c'est la mort, et ce qui est l'avant-goût et la petite monnaie de la mort."

There is a story that Goethe in youth wrote the exquisite poem:

"Ueber alle Gipfeln ist ruh"

which ends on the sombre note

"Warte nur balde, *ruhest du auch*"

It is said that at a much older age he went back to the place which had inspired these lines; the people he had loved had died and he felt old and sad and wept bitterly. I, who have survived two wars, am a widow and have lost my home, know just how he felt. Age has little use for romantic pessimism.

It would be pleasant to relate that after my readings of Amiel and Pascal that I became a philosopher. I should like to record that I have acquired honorary recognitions in that line—I have received two degrees, one from McGill University and one from Toronto University, and I did address a full session of the University of Toronto, on "The Role of the Amateur in History", but alas these are the sum of my academic distinctions.

As a girl I must have lived a strenuous mental double life, as I was flung into that most difficult of worlds, London society of the early years of this century. Society was small at that time, a great many of the people who composed it being related by blood or marriage; and the most glittering prizes were in the hands of those people who lived for part of the year in large London houses, and for the rest in even larger houses on their country estates.

I went recently to see an Irish actor in his one-man performance of *The Importance of Being Oscar*. He acted the scene in which Lady Bracknell cross-questions Ernest Worthing on his worldly prospects. It struck me forcibly that his version of Lady Bracknell was exactly like some dowagers I remember, although they did not have so much verbal wit.

Lady Catherine de Burgh had also some points in common with some people in Edwardian days, so I suppose women like this cropped up over and over again in the years intervening between Jane Austen and Oscar Wilde—formidable dowagers, who scrutinised with eagle eyes the antecedents of the young men on their dinner and ball lists.

These dowagers had often been beautiful and charming when they were younger, and had at some point it was whispered (or openly said) thrown their caps over the moon. But when they grew old their looks were apt to be rugged. There were few aids to beauty then and the clothes they wore were expensive, ugly and unbecoming. They took a stand on being *alarming* (this was a word much bandied about in those days), and would stare formidably through lorgnettes. I think they felt that to be powerful and frightening was a substitute for being young and charming. This seems strange now, but in my recollection it was so. Young, shy people had to bear with being snubbed, as frequently had the middle-aged and elderly who were not smart or influential. But it is only fair to say that some dowagers were delightfully kind, and charmed people instead of frightening them.

Every family had a bugbear, a member of the older generation who consistently criticised youthful behaviour. We had one such distant cousin, and I remember that my mother, who seldom saw her and thought her stupid, would say when my sister and I had committed some mild blunder: "What *would* Mary X say if she heard about this?" Stupidity often is a terribly potent force.

For all my philosophical readings I was the product of my world and the circumstances of my life. I soon developed a love of social life with parties and dancing. I even enjoyed what was then called a "drum", a sort of party where men and women were crowded together in a room and tried to talk to each other, making parrot-house sounds, as do the guests at a modern cocktail party. It was held late in the evening, after dinner, and was considered by most people a boring duty, a sort of sweep-up of acquaintances. But drums had their points all the same—at least to a young person who was eager to see people, coiffures, and clothes, and not to be called upon to make much contribution.

One of my mother's friends said to her that they thought I was a nice normal girl, and I suppose I was; but when she repeated this to me I was much offended. "I suppose he means I'm dull," I retorted huffily. My mother tried to explain that normality need not necessarily imply dullness, but I still was not pleased!

As I look back, our attitudes are amazing. It caused me no surprise when my sister wrote to me and said, "I expect the Boer War will spoil the London season." It did spoil it. There were very few entertainments, other than charitable bazaars for the soldiers' comforts (if they could be called

III.   The Author

IV.   Maud Grosvenor—Mrs. Maurice Glyn

entertainments). The war was very remote to us—it had none of the hourly pressures on the nerves of two more recent world wars, as a result of radio communications. There was a time coming when our lives would be shaken and our foundations undermined beyond the comprehension of anyone then living.

What the Boer War did do was severely to impair our national complacency about our armed forces, our generals, and our capacity to wage a successful war against a small nation.

I remember being ill with 'flu during a week of British defeats, the heavy unhappiness which hung over me and the whole of our house and the sense of outraged surprise that went with it. The generals were blamed, the War Office was anathematised for inefficiency, and the war was the major topic discussed by our elders.

We young people felt bewildered and uncertain. Our history books had played down our failures, so that our past seemed one long success story. The Crimean War was mentioned only for the valour of the Charge of the Light Brigade. The maps of the world had an overwhelming area of British colouring, and we felt the world had altered and we could not understand the significance of our defeats in South Africa. Like all younger people we enjoyed dramatic happenings and we got a certain excitement about it all; but for our elders life was never the same again.

I HAVE been reading Roger Fulford's excellent essay on King Edward the Seventh,* written with great insight and urbanity. It has brought me some amusing recollections.

The attitude of my family to royalty was a curiously aloof one. My grandfather, Lord Ebury, had been a member of the Prince Consort's Household and my grandmother's brother, Gerald Wellesley, who was Dean of Windsor, had been greatly liked and trusted by Queen Victoria. But I never heard any gossip about the Royal Family. Later on when I was grown up in Edwardian days my mother remarked that she thought any gossip about royalty was rather vulgar, or, worse still, boring, and like the servants' hall.

We did the usual things, however. I went to Court balls after being presented at Court, and I saw Queen Alexandra, who looked majestically beautiful in a gold dress with wonderful jewels. I suffered all the usual misgivings of a debutante, fearing that my train would catch on something, or that I should stumble and fall ignominiously at Their Majesties' feet; but all was well. I made my curtsey, was smiled at by the Queen, and my train was flung over my arm by a court official as I walked backwards into the supper room feeling relieved and elated.

In spite of my mother's strictness, gossip was always in the air. A friend of my mother, Lady Troubridge, told us of her talk with the King somewhere in the South of France. She left him laughing and amused as she was a woman of great charm who excelled in light conversation. In spite of his

* In *Edwardian England, 1901–1910;* Oxford University Press, 1964.

reputation for geniality it was no easy task to amuse the King, and he had a way of drumming with his fingers on the arms of his chair when he was bored. However, on this occasion he was amused, and Mrs. Keppel came in and asked what they had been talking about that had actually made H.M. laugh.

I once saw Mrs. Keppel at a ball at the Rothschilds' house in Piccadilly, and I was disappointed in her looks, though she must have had some beauty. She wore a tiara which, if my memory serves me right, was a mass of diamonds made up of a pattern of loops and curves. Mrs. Keppel must have had an enduring charm for she was much praised for her good humour and kindness. Her life cannot have been an easy one, and yet I remember Lady Troubridge saying of her that Alice Keppel never forgot a friend or downed an enemy.

I found a letter some years ago from my aunt, Lady Lovelace. Alas, it has vanished, but I can remember the gist of it. "We have a time of it here (Marienbad) dodging H.R.H. (of whom my Uncle Ralph Lovelace disapproved) behind skinny little trees."

My uncle and aunt were both short in stature and the reverse of slim, and this must have been a difficult operation. Mary Lovelace, who had a more traditional outlook on life than her husband, felt that these tree-dodgings showed a lack of respect for royalty by a member of the peerage. But she loyally followed her husband's lead and continued dodging behind skinny little trees when H.R.H. came in sight.

Uncle Ralph Lovelace was not Byron's grandson for nothing. He could look gloomy or thunderous, and it was wise not to take a chance on his manners. He was a recluse and a fine scholar and writer. He was kind to his nieces, who felt an awed affection for him, but his temper was fiery and unpredictable.

My aunt Mary and her husband, Ralph Lovelace, lived a

strange and secluded life on their two properties—Ockham Park in Surrey, a Hawksmoor house surrounded by spreading lawns shaded by spreading cedar trees, and Ashley Coombe near Porlock, a smaller house with wonderful views and dense woods which stretched for miles along an arm of the sea. They also had an imposing terra-cotta coloured house in London at the corner of the Embankment and Swan Walk—and they went abroad to small inns in Switzerland as my uncle was a noted mountaineer.

My aunt, who was my mother's elder sister, married Ralph Lovelace when she was thirty-two. He had been brought up by his grandmother, Lady Byron, and he championed her all his life. My aunt, who had lived in a large cheerful and artistic family, had to endure a quiet and ingrown existence. She was forced to listen to tales of the wickedness of Byron's publishers and she lived to be heavily involved in squabbles about wills and inheritances.

Ralph Lovelace wrote after years of work and thought a privately printed book called *Astarte*, purporting to tell the ultimate truth about Byron and Augusta Leigh. But he failed in this as the book, though it had fine passages in it, was obscure and vitriolic.

I have said that his temper was unpredictable. We children were warned never to mention Byron at meals. As we knew nothing about the poet and cared less, this was easy but it had the effect of reducing us to complete silence. Uncle Ralph didn't care much for children, but he was kind to all his wife's nieces and nephews and we accorded him a kind of awed reverence. When I was growing up and he found that I loved books he would bring me armfuls of volumes and pile them up on the floor round me. He was stocky in figure, had untidy dark hair and wore eccentric clothes.

My aunt was a forceful character whose strange and lonely life caused her opinions to be frozen into the attitudes of her youth. She thought young people silly and unwise in most of the things they said and did, and she did not hesitate to criticise our clothes and our behaviour. We listened in sullen silence when she talked about our dresses as we considered her own taste in clothes to be odd and deplorable. She scolded me once for wearing a green dress at Ockham. "Green," she said, "should never be worn in the country, where what with the trees and the grass there is so much greenness about."

She had started life wanting to be an artist, but did not consider that she had enough talent to go on with this. She was a lifelong friend of Evelyn de Morgan; she hung Wentworth House in London with her pictures. Her family had not much regard for them, although they respected Evelyn de Morgan as a hard-working and dedicated artist. These pictures are now coming into favour and I wish their painter could know of this, as she worked so faithfully for so many years without success. Aunt Mary held strong views about the necessity of helping the artists of her date and age, and she inveighed against the many people who bought old masters or hung reproductions on their walls. She fostered arts and crafts societies and helped poor artists.

One of her great joys in life was her parrots. She had a large and solemn cockatoo called William of Ockham who either sat on a perch or suddenly launched himself into the air. But she always had with her one or two little green parrots of whom she went in awe. They had uncertain tempers and you could expect no sympathy from my aunt if they disliked you. They roamed under the table during meals and one of them once bit my ankle severely. "I don't like cowardice about parrots," my aunt remarked when I complained about this.

Aunt Mary was not very pleased about my engagement to John Buchan. She had hoped for a nephew who possessed a large country house standing in a park. But both my husband and she could recognise qualities of heart and mind, and they became fast friends, and we stayed with her after her widowhood both in the country and at Wentworth House. She grew mellower with age and I grew more understanding of her points of view and her prejudices.

Many of my contemporaries who had been brought up in the strictest sect of young ladyhood rebelled against their enforced idleness and complained to their friends. My cousin, Hilda Lyttleton, said bitterly to me one day, "I want to do something better than rush up and down Oxford Street hunting for beastly pieces of tulle." The explanation of this rather cryptic remark lay in the fact that her mother, and mine as well, strove economically to revive old and faded dresses with bits of lace, chiffon and tulle, which in fact did not succeed in doing anything except give the dress in question a slightly messy and muddled appearance.

Today, younger people who delight in the style and finish of Cecil Beaton's designs in *My Fair Lady*, imagine that we looked like this all the time; perhaps we did occasionally at Ascot or a ball, but in ordinary life our clothes were often bitty and covered with useless ornaments.

Hilda Lyttleton married Arthur Grenfell and became a stepmother and mother of four daughters. After her marriage she wore distinguished clothes. Looking back I can see her wearing tea-gowns made by the Italian dress designer Fortuny, whose fanciful but lovely dresses were all the rage in those days. He made for her long straight garments of artfully pleated satin held at neck, wrists and waist by strings of small iridescent shells. Fortuny wished his clients to look like the ladies in Italian pictures; his dresses suited Hilda to perfection and no messy or irrelevant ornament was there. The Grenfells lived in Roehampton House, a worthy setting for a magnificent ball which they gave, where Hilda wearing a tiara and a white and gold dress was a sight to see for all who admired her special kind of beauty.

As the years went by she had a fine record of work for the Young Women's Christian Association. She became their National President and undertook a highly perilous journey in the Second World War up to a battle front in the Far East to visit their clubs. Perhaps her visits to the Oxford Street shops may have helped to add to her experience of people, and the time spent there had not been a total loss.

A Scottish friend of mine startled her relations by taking a course in laundry. In the Edinburgh of those days household washing was done at home and behind those large, stately houses in crescents or squares, sheets hung on poles in the narrow sloping back "greens" as they were called. But a young married woman taking a course in laundry was considered odd by her elders. "So unnecessary," they said, "when you can always get someone in to do it."

It was always better to devote yourself to improving your mind; always providing you had a mind to improve. Mind improvement was taken seriously. But in case there might be a horrid suggestion of the blue-stocking about it, learning had to be carried lightly and not overstressed. Men were supposed to be shy of cleverness, though not all were. I am sure that our partners would have welcomed more signs of intelligence on the part of the girls they danced with whose conversation was usually limited to the floor and the band. Our elders had a strange *mystique* about what girls should and should not do. The mixture of muddle and cloud-cuckoo-land in which they lived makes an odd picture.

It is all the more strange because new ideas were taking shape in a world that was changing all the time, and the people we lived among were not stupid even if they chose to appear so. They in fact reduced themselves to the level of the

stupidest people while carefully concealing their own intellectual activities. This may perhaps have stemmed from the
fact that the New Woman, as portrayed in *Punch* wearing
knickerbockers and with closely cropped hair, was beginning
to make herself heard. Stupider people equated intellectual
women with those who wore floppy dark green Liberty
dresses, strings of beads and flat-heeled shoes. There were of
course the Souls, the fashionable intellectuals who dressed
with a kind of aesthetic smartness of their own. But they too
were a little suspect as not conforming to the social game.

The social life of London was in the hands of women who
regarded it as something outside ordinary life, as an affair of
the right people supported by the best bands, stacks of
Malmaison carnations, and enough dancing men—always an
anxious consideration, as young men were tricky undepen-
dable creatures. The ordeal that we girls faced at a ball is
something incomprehensible today. It was also incomprehensible to our daughters in the 1920s when the idea of
dinners before dances came in, and a girl would be accompanied to a dance by a young man who was her "partner".
In my youth those of us who had not attracted a sufficient
quota of partners sat on the chaperone's bench. The chaper-
ones kindly tried to talk to us and we tried to look gay and
animated, but it was painfully obvious that we deserved that
horrid word "wall-flowers". I was perhaps lucky as my
mother in a quiet way entertained a good deal and many
young men came to the house; but there were evenings with
very painful memories even now, though I can smile at my
recollections of the bitterness of those moments.

My mother went sometimes for refreshment of spirit to
see Charles Booth and his wife, who had a house in Great
Cumberland Place. Charles Booth was chairman of the Booth
Line, a shipping company. He devoted much time and no
inconsiderable amount of money to statistical enquiries into

social questions. He embodied many of his results in several volumes of a book called *The Life and Labour of People in London*. It contains a striking series of maps in which the varying degrees of poverty are represented street by street. Charles Booth had been a friend of my father's, and my father had helped him by finding out the backgrounds of the servants who worked in various London clubs.

Charles Booth and his enchanting wife never bothered about the arid stretches of London society, and at their house my mother met men and women who talked frankly and thought deeply about social questions.

A younger friend of mine, Constance Lane, a charming artist, combined London dances with hard work. She was a clergyman's daughter and has left a delightful fragment of prose called *The Rectories*. I quote briefly from it as her experiences of Edwardian youth were somewhat different from mine. She describes the dances she went to: ". . . the slow waltzing with long steps, the long white gloves worn to the elbow, our hair done with little curls heaped high or kept in place by a grecian wreath of gold leaves or perhaps a graceful wave on the forehead. There were butterflies and wall-flowers. I do not remember being one or the other but a friend once said, 'It's fun taking you out, you always look so happy all the time'."

Her conversation at balls was more intellectual than mine. "Talk," she says, "was a little stilted and I was overjoyed when someone would talk about Turner's paintings or Plato. . . ." She goes on to say, "One heard a good deal about the wrong people getting into society, but there were plenty of right ones to go on with, and didn't they know it. Some of the right ones were quite poor, and took rooms in Ebury Street. But I think the mothers and daughters enjoyed themselves parading in the Park on Sundays after tea, and meeting their old friends. The elm trees just in green leaf throwing becoming shadows over old and young in toppers and feather boas and picture hats."

Constance went to the Slade school. "Sir Hugh Lane gave me an introduction to Professor Tonks who ruled the Slade in all his later glory." She writes: "I have no reason to question his supremacy for I found him a fine teacher and a delightful person. Against the greys and dirty greens of the walls of the art-room I see him advancing in his grey suit, tall and bony, the upper part of his face eagle-like, the lower part having a slightly long-suffering and amused look, as of an observer. His autocratic manner did not alarm me and his disquisitions on drawings to new students really did open my eyes and describe a method.

"Pinafored girl students moved about the class-rooms, a smell of oil paint pervaded everywhere, and robust male students lounged and argued. Every face and character seemed to stand out against the olive green paint and grey stone of the Slade. It was a world of its own with Brown, the Head Tonks, Russell, and Child, the secretary, not to speak of Wilson Steer who taught painting.

"My evenings were spent among relations for I was usually staying in Manchester Square with the Reginald Talbots. Their house was well appointed and they often entertained remarkable people. Although properly impressed with Empire builders and persons of high degree I was generally too tired and sleepy after a day's work at the Slade to enter into an older world.

"Still it made interesting contrasts. The main problem seemed to be getting clean in time for dinner. Whether to be dirty and punctual or clean and late? I am sorry to say that I generally chose the latter. These were the days of good service and the Talbots' butler, Mr. Fripp, was the perfect butler. His head was a shining ostrich egg, his manner a blend of fatherliness, observation and pomposity. He adored his masters, and they him, and any domestic who worked under his care learned the proper ritual of the dining-room.

"To me he was ever kind, and when I was given what my hostess called 'cats' meat', *i.e.* an informal supper, it was brought up to my room by Fripp, punctual and beautifully arranged. I liked those meals when my elders were out and I could browse among the bookshelves."

Constance Lane had beauty, vitality and charm. She died, alas, untimely, leaving some charming pictures and a vivid memory in the minds of those who knew her.

IN the decade about which I write people of moderate means managed to live in large inconvenient houses involving domestic problems which strike chill to our hearts, unnerved as we are by present-day decline in domestic service. I must often have lunched and dined in such houses—London before its bombing presented acres of terraced houses, interspersed with squares, surrounded by what we should now call mansions, of almost unbroken uniformity.

These not rich people supported existence without apparent misgivings, in houses with front steps, area steps, breakneck kitchen stairs, formidable front stairs with at least three half-landings. Up and down them passed all day processions of tradesmen delivering food and coal and coke, maids carrying up trays for the dining-room, scuttles for the bedroom fires and brass cans of hot water, lamps to light the rooms, and frequently, up to the top storey but one, nursery and schoolroom meals.

Two younger members of my family live today in a flat perched high in a house just off the Cromwell Road, in elegant tall rooms that must once have been the children's and servants' quarters. This was never a "smart" neighbourhood. The people who occupied these houses were not "in society", had probably no special pretensions and could afford few servants. When I first visited my family I was confronted by what seemed to be an Everest of stairs—what sort of people, I wondered, had lived in this house and managed to keep it reasonably clean and warm? I do not know the answer. I suspect that the master of the house was a

V. Cycling in Hyde Park

VI.   A View up Park Lane

professional man, a doctor, a lawyer, a soldier, perhaps a Civil Servant.

What was it like to live in such a house, I wondered—did the mistress of the house lend a hand, or keep most of the rooms not actually in use under dust-sheets?

London is a much cleaner place than it was once. In my youth there were fogs in winter with showers of grimy soot flakes. It was impossible for a cab driver or a pedestrian to see more than a foot or so through the impenetrable blackness that descended, lightening here and there to sulphurous yellow with the consistency of inky soup. I remember an agonising evening when I was going to a much-looked-forward-to mid-Lent dance (many hostesses did not give parties in Lent and this was the week called in France *mi-carême*). My mother was understandably nervous about venturing out in the "pea soup" murk—but mercifully it lifted sufficiently to allow us to go.

The cleaning of a house after a fog presented endless problems. However tightly the windows were kept shut, greasy dirt got in everywhere, clinging persistently to curtains and covers, tarnishing brass and silver and filling our lungs with foul vapours. In spacious rooms with elaborate cornices a velvety film of black settled on the mouldings.

All this must greatly have added to the difficulties of running such a house as I have described, staffed perhaps by a cook with varicose veins, an anaemic housemaid and a parlourmaid who had her hands full trying to keep the massive and bulbous silver of the period bright.

Stresses and strains in human life differ from generation to generation, but at least we are spared the toil of keeping up appearances, and can look on these Edwardian labour-making houses without envy, but with a good deal of respect for those who, apparently effortlessly, lived in them.

Some social usages of these times are amusing to recall,

I opened *Edwardian England* at Miss Marghanita Laski's article on social customs and laughed to think that the, to me, familiar pattern of life seems as unreal to the young of to-day as a fantasy dreamed up by Lewis Carroll. As I read, the presence of the Frog Footman seemed to pervade the room. I quote: "The first desideratum was to obtain cards, for a lady they should be thickish, for a gentleman small and thin . . . the strict rules as to who left cards on whom and how and when, would demand more space then can be spared. A lady who has met another lady at a dinner-party or at afternoon tea, should not leave cards until further meetings have enabled her to feel sure that her acquaintance is desired. . . . Calling in this period was almost entirely confined to afternoon calls made after three o'clock. . . ."

The rules were not, after all, so complicated. The caller asked if the lady of the house was "at home"; if the answer was no, meaning either that she was out or that she did not choose to receive, the caller dropped her cards on to a silver salver brought out by the footman or parlourmaid, without leaving her carriage. One corner of the card was lightly turned up to show that she had called in person.

My recollections of this social activity are patchy because my mother and I were equally bored by it. My mother was a lazy "caller" and much preferred spending the afternoon in her studio. However, as she had two daughters to launch into the social world of London, from time to time she unwillingly awoke to her responsibilities, hired a brougham and set out with me, armed with a slim card case. Grimly we worked our way through the list of those who should be called on, putting up a silent prayer that no one would be at home. If they were, that meant spending half an hour in polite conversation, balancing a tea-cup; the "polishing off" process would thus be slowed up, which meant wasting another precious afternoon another day.

My mother's sisters had houses in York Terrace, in Chelsea, and in Victoria, and we as children were shuffled between them as and how it suited our elders' convenience. We adored Moor Park with its endless pleasances, and to us the London parks (Hyde Park which was nearest to Grosvenor Street, was "The Park"), were merely dehydrated versions of the country, with low railings where hedges should have been. The bark of the London trees was grimy black, and melancholy sheep stood in the middle distance weighed down by sooty fleeces.

On Sundays ladies sat at home behind their tea-tables and men, young and not so young, called on them, afterwards adjourning to Hyde Park to meet their friends. Sunday was the day for this sort of activity, after church and before Sunday luncheon being an especially favoured time. By taking part in this ritual people not "in society" believed they became part of the London social scene. It was all very pleasant and ephemeral this carrying on of conversations with the shimmer of flirtation on the surface of light talk and laughter—impossible to recreate as is the Edwardian era itself.

The London parks have no elegance for me now. They are too tightly packed on fine days, too desolate and empty on wet ones.

My sister and I found walks in the Park a penance and much preferred the amusement of shop windows. Park Lane, now a ceaselessly pouring river of traffic, presented to our childish eyes a series of dull blank garden walls behind which the great houses slumbered with most of the blinds drawn. Trees could be seen over the tops of the walls but very little else. Grosvenor House, through whose gates on Upper Grosvenor Street smart equipages drove out and in, was like this. In the little streets and alleys that linked quiet residential Grosvenor Street with bustling Oxford Street, lived pensioned-off dependants of the Grosvenor family, to whom we took our boots to be mended, or from whom we bought vegetables, or who came in to caretake and oblige when the London house was shut up for the summer holidays.

We would have been contemptuous of anyone who had told us that Park Lane had not so long before been a real lane down which cows were driven; or that the quarter of London in which we lived had still much in common with a village in the country.

After my marriage, before the birth of our first child, when we lived in Hyde Park Square, the Park became the setting for many happy evening strolls after my husband came home from his office, and on the morning of my daughter's birth I walked into the Park accompanied by my sister. She read aloud to me Robert Louis Stevenson's story *The Suicide Club*. We were both absorbed in it, when my mother suddenly descended on us, removed the book with a firm gesture and escorted me home.

After our two elder children were born, the Park acquired a certain value and I grew fond of it. Children must have their quota of fresh air and our Nannie spent hours pushing the heavy old-fashioned pram of Edwardian days with its high tussore canopy. The mother (a weaker vessel) deputised for her on her days off, often feeling diminished and ashamed when she had to slump exhausted on the nearest seat, and begin to joggle the pram in the hope that the baby would be deceived into thinking that it was still in motion. No Nannie would have deigned to sit alone on the accessible seat where the mother so gladly sank to rest. Nannie always pushed on to a bench where a row of other Nannies were already seated. The Park was quartered into the beats of the Bayswater Nannies, the Mayfair Nannies, the Belgravia Nannies, and in Kensington Gardens the Nannies of that ilk. When they had settled down, conversation would run something like this:

"She asked me to go downstairs to supper. I said I couldn't

demean myself. The nursery-maid can bring up my tray, I said."

"My nursery-maid wouldn't like *that*."

"My nursery-maid does what I tell her."

The habits and peculiarities of the family were milled over in jerky bursts of talk. Only mothers were discussed—fathers being necessary but rather remote figures. Elder brothers and sisters were usually dismissed as uninteresting unless they had a slavish devotion to the smaller children of the family, and frankly preferred the atmosphere of the nursery they had left to that of the drawing-room or the library. In fact to the parent sitting unobserved on a nearby green chair, the Nannies' talk was a salutary lesson. Seeing ourselves as others see us, is an experience not often granted to the ordinary mortal, and though eavesdroppers seldom hear any good of themselves they learn something of value.

I have a delightful recollection of our Nannie telling me about a baby who was strangely born with a full quota of teeth. This had, she said, caused great comment amongst the assembled Nannies—in fact, she added, "It was the talk of the Park".

Presently the Nannies would rise to their feet and with their hard black hats, grey-stockinged legs and their feet in sensible low-heeled black shoes, would disperse to their various homes, pushing their prams, a drab, patient procession. The prams would be hauled up front steps into spacious or narrow halls, and the children dragged and carried up flights of stairs to the nurseries by panting nursery-maids.

At their worst Nannies could be arbitrary, touchy and cross, at their best loving and easy to do with, and kindly and maternal in the best sense, unstinting in devotion to their charges. The Victorian and Edwardian Nannie gave their charges a standard of behaviour which served these children in later life in good stead.

"Say grace properly, don't mumble. You're talking to God."

"Say please *and* thank you."

"No passing personal remarks, now."

"Don't snatch, ask nicely. Let the visitor have your train (or doll)."

"Don't listen to things (*i.e.* grown-up conversation) that you're not meant to hear."

"Behave or not at all."

Many an adult has found these nebulous maxims useful if difficult to carry out in later life, but none the less they set a standard.

In the twilight when the fireguard in front of a coal fire was draped with airing garments, Nannies would tell marvellous stories of their homes and childhood doings, giving the richer child a glimpse of a rural childhood in a small cottage in village or in mining town, where conditions had hardly changed since the Industrial Revolution. The generations who were in charge of Nannies have something stamped on them in the way of behaviour which can never come again, a sense of the proper way in which to conduct life, from the right way to tie up a shoelace—that first victory over inanimate matter—to the refusal or acceptance of a proposal of marriage.

The nursery world functioned strictly by the tick of a large bald-faced clock on the mantelpiece. Nursery life cemented solidarity between brothers and sisters. Shared games played on a shabby carpet (or battered linoleum) or an ink-stained table cloth, are memories common to all of us who had a like upbringing, in a world sealed off by steep stairs, governed by inexorable routine.

Nannies have their place in the social history of this country, just as the governess has found her place in its literature. It is amusing to think that the most famous of all is that four-footed charmer, that model of integrity and devotion, "Nanna" in *Peter Pan*. Perhaps Barrie was right, and the nicest kind of dog and the best kind of Nannie have much in common.

NEXT to a dance, a little party for the play was our most elegant occasion. Our elders gave the preliminary dinner party inviting the young men we were seeing at the moment, and we wore for our satisfaction our very nicest clothes, short of our best ball dresses, and did our hair with particular care, since in the theatre only our heads were noticeable.

In those happier days plays never began before 8.30 and sometimes 8.45—plenty of time to enjoy dinner and share the peculiar thrill that the theatre shed over us for hours before and after a performance. (Matinees were not the same; one always felt slightly guilty at enjoying oneself in the afternoon.) Over one's evening dress, one wore a borrowed velvet cloak belonging to an aunt and carried one's handkerchief in a small velvet bag drawn up with a cord.

There was a moment of pleasurable panic when the hansom was held up by the traffic in Piccadilly—the light from gas lamps showed smiling happy anxious faces in similar situations all round us. All London seemed bent on "going to the play" between the hours of eight and nine.

Theatres were all built to much the same design, red-carpeted, gilt-encrusted, with nameless deities painted on the proscenium arch and ceiling, which were upheld by fully-clothed caryatids or discreetly draped cherubs.

Once we had rustled into our seats and dipped into the programmes which our young men bought for us, to make sure that Charles Wyndham or George Alexander were not being replaced by their understudies that night, we would look cautiously round, appraise the coiffures and jewels in the stalls, and boxes, and thrill to the rising excitement as the orchestra filed in and began to tune up.

Theatres, like everything else that once seemed permanent and stable, have changed. The décor tends to be stark—gone the Olympian deities with a bloom of dust on their rounded limbs, and sometimes even there is no curtain, giving one an uneasy feeling of having wandered into the wrong bedroom. Enchantment was present in those days I write of, and reached an almost unbearable pitch when the footlights went up and the fringed red velvet curtains quivered in the yellow glow.

Going to the play in Edwardian days was a social occasion, a graceful affair; and what one saw acted was apt to be graceful too. The theatre was a place where one went to be entertained. No one was trying to teach us anything or promote a particular point of view.

Wilde and Pinero and Henry Arthur Jones, deploying wit in their mannered comedies, did not feel it necessary to point a moral; that was to come in with Galsworthy, and of course with Bernard Shaw, whose main preoccupation was with the defects in the English character, which he showed up brilliantly, lengthily, sometimes intolerably tediously, pricking us into a kind of national self-awareness which was far from being to our advantage.

Being young and unsophisticated, we didn't go to the theatre in a critical spirit, but to have an altogether enjoyable outing, often coupled with mild—or if lucky enough to be sitting in a box, ardent—flirtation.

We loved what we called screaming farces and gay light-hearted musical comedies like *San Toy* or *The Geisha Girl*. Later, when I was married, I saw Lily Elsie in *The Merry Widow* and her tea-rose loveliness added a new dimension to the evening's enjoyment.

THE EDWARDIAN LADY AT THE THEATRE

I can remember discussion as to whether Marie Tempest would ever succeed as an actress, as she was thought by us to be extremely plain, with her funny little pug-like face, and dumpy figure. Actresses in those days were expected to be either pretty or graceful, talent was a secondary consideration. However her outstanding artistry soon won her her rightful place as one of our most accomplished actresses. We loved her, and someone who had been in Paris remarked that the actresses there, although outstanding in their art, were not particularly blessed by good looks, so that helped too. (I don't know whether this statement was true or false!) Criticism of plays and actors was not informed or professional. We "liked" this one, and "didn't like" that one, "adored" someone else.

It was fun to fall in love with one of the actors, and as far as I can remember the second actor who took my fancy was an American, William Gillette. He was a tall man with a rather gaunt interesting face. My first love had been in my schoolroom days, a German actor called Josef Kainz whom I saw in Berlin. His performance of John the Baptist still remains with me as one of the finest things I ever saw, and for years I cherished two photographs of him.

I wish now that I had seen Irving in his hey-day and Sarah Bernhardt in hers, and not when they were both ageing. Sarah's performance of the tragic young Duke de Reichstadt in Rostand's *L'Aiglon* was something to see though; even old, lame and heavily corseted as she was. She made you realise his sorrow to the full. Her voice was still vibrating and lovely, and her burning eyes dominated her ageing rouged face; it is something to remember that one has seen her, and in a part which no actress of today would dare to attempt.

It is an arguable point whether going to see famous artists at the end of their careers is really a good idea. I took my young daughter to see Eleonora Duse in one of her last performances in England in Ibsen's *Ghosts*. I felt sad because I had seen Duse in her younger days, and there was not much left of her magic beyond the hollow mournful voice, and the still beautiful hands. Shaw said of her that she always used some part of her body to illustrate the sort of character she was portraying—eyes, chin, shoulders, arms, hands, back, even feet. On this last occasion of all, she put the whole of Mrs. Alving's tragedy into one comprehensive gesture of those wonderful white hands that seemed to embody the past, the present and the future.

I remember the American actress Elizabeth Robins, of whom I have written elsewhere, taking me to see some Ibsen plays in German. My German wasn't quite good enough to grasp the finer shades of meaning, but the stagecraft of Ibsen and the taut interest of the stories came through to me, giving me an appetite for something more than light comedy. What is more, the players were completely audible to the farthest limits of the auditorium. What Noël Coward has called the "scratch and mumble brigade" had not come into being, and I can't recall actors ever turning their back on an audience.

In the long roll of plays we enjoyed I find myself pre-eminently remembering *Peter Pan*, which burst on us all as the work of genius it was. I have seen it now over and over again with my children and grandchildren, and I never fail to be struck by its depth of fancy and imagination. I wince a bit always, as I did when I first saw it, at the bits about mother-love which have a sort of searching sentimentality, calculated to make any mother feel slightly sick. The rest of the magnificent fantasy is undimmed and I still enjoy it.

To aid my recollections I have leafed over the pages of the admirably helpful volumes of the Annual Register. The writers of these compilations unexpectedly charm by the flatness of their comments; and surprise one with shrewd assessments of events and people.

In 1905 the Annual Register remarks that Shaw had become one of the most distinguished of English playwrights. *Man and Superman*, *You Never Can Tell*, and *Major Barbara* were put on at the Royal Court Theatre.

In 1906 I saw Shaw's *The Doctor's Dilemma* with Granville Barker as Louis Dubedat and Lilla McCarthy as his wife. A lady rose up in the stalls and left the theatre during Louis Dubedat's mock creed, protesting loudly. The Annual Register comments that "Granville Barker could not bring Louis Dubedat to life, but that he made him amusing and less repulsive than anyone else could have done—because Louis has the irresponsibility of genius joined to the practical cunning of street arab."

In later life I formed two perfect friendships—with Harley Granville-Barker and his second wife, which continued through the years till both of them died. Much has been written about Harley as the author of *Prefaces to Shakespeare*, and as a playwright and a producer of plays. I should like to add to this a small tribute to his gentle humour, and to the way he never controlled any conversation by laying down the law, but was one of those rare people who draw out other people's ideas and make the best and most illuminating talk seem easy and delightful. At the time of which I write he was embarking on the Vedrenne-Barker adventure in management at the Royal Court Theatre which was to make theatrical history.

It is hard to explain to any playgoer of today the kind of breakthrough this management was to the theatre-goers of the Edwardian age. Instead of the lightness and gay triviality which had flowed over us, we were confronted by mockery, and pricked into thought. One couldn't *love* a Shaw play, but one could be stung into awareness of many things by it; and Shakespeare was freed from the over-elaboration with which Tree and Irving had weighed down their productions, and made to live.

Gilbert Murray's translation of the *Hippolytus* marked an era in my life. Forbes Robertson's was the most satisfying Hamlet I have ever seen. I had been taken to see it by two young men, and not knowing the play it struck me with enormous force; I went home weeping bitterly, to the amazement of my companions who were members of the Brigade of Guards. I became a haunter of the Court Theatre and saw the plays there as often as I could manage.

Barrie's plays were also always good entertainment—I went with my Scotch family-in-law to see *What Every Woman Knows* and remember the way they laughed at the authentic Scotchness of it. I can recall vividly his little masterpiece, *The Twelve Pound Look*, and Hilda Trevelyan's performance in it.

All the players I write about in the plays we saw are dead and gone—but some of the plays live on to be revived and critically assessed by the present generation, who as a matter of fact derive a great many of their own ideas from them in spite of the differences in humour, costumes, and general attitudes.

I often think of these old theatre days, and wish I could see plays again which I saw when they were new minted and fresh, when I sat gripping the arm of my stall wondering what would come next and where the following twist and turn of the plot would take us, absolutely absorbed, totally involved. The ghosts pass before me—Gerald du Maurier, Cyril Maude, Charles Hawtrey, Irene and Violet Vanbrugh, Marie Tempest, Martin Harvey in *The Only Way*, Lily Brayton and Oscar Asche in *The Taming of the Shrew*, Pelissier in *The Follies* with a blond wig and a long riding habit, cracking a hunting crop as Lady Di in his parody of a sporting drama at Drury Lane.

Gone too are many of the theatres themselves, and apparently gone for ever the good-mannered ready-to-be-pleased attitude of audiences who dressed with care, deeming it an incivility to the actors to do less, thus contributing their personal share to the evening's entertainment. The dissolving television screen has perhaps made us lazy—at all events the theatres now seem to me to be full of people who do not trouble to make going to the play an occasion.

OUR elders had strange taboos. Almost all French books were banned except for innocuous tales like Halévy's *Mon Oncle et mon Curé* and *Princesse*. Erckmann-Chatrian, René Bazin and Alphonse Daudet were permitted, but the glories of Balzac and de Maupassant and the supreme Flaubert were reserved for the married woman. *Le Rouge et Noir* and *La Chartreuse de Parme* of Stendhal were unwillingly conceded as being so difficult to get through that any improprieties would probably pass unperceived. We read Dumas Père in French; Dumas Fils not at all.

Our elders were over-cautious in setting these taboos. Left to browse, we innocent creatures would have taken no possible harm. No doubt they thought they were protecting us from the contagion of the world's Slow Stain—but just as they forbade our enjoyment of the illuminatingly comic world of Feydeau, or the sophistication of Sudermann and Schnitzler in the theatre, so they controlled our reading, and sought to keep us splashing indefinitely in the shallows of adolescence. But the issues in Ibsen are fundamental, and it occurred to no one to forbid us the reading of eighteenth-century novels, or of Gibbon or Richard Burton; we were therefore at liberty to put two and two together as best we might. I remember pointless discussions raging over my head as to whether I should be allowed to read *The Visits of Elizabeth* by Elinor Glyn. I managed a surreptitious look at it and could see no double meanings, though I was on the look-out for them. It seemed to me quite amusing but ordinary sort of stuff and rather silly. Strangely I was allowed to read *The Mill on the Floss* and *Silas Marner*, but not *Adam Bede*—one supposes because of the very soberly and allusively-treated seduction scene in it.

In 1903 the Annual Register solemnly states that "few poets have caught the popular taste, on the other hand there is more demand for biography". In this year Morley's *Life of Gladstone* came out (alas, I have never attempted to read it), also *Human Personality and Survival after Death* by Frederick Myers. He had been a friend of my father and I did read this with considerable interest. Lord Haldane gave my mother his book *The Pathway to Reality*, and several years later, helped by my future husband, I did try to understand it, but gave it up, feeling that metaphysics were not a pathway I could comfortably tread.

The Annual Register has no use for authors who indulge in "the perverse habit of placing their men and women in surroundings of Park Lane or Poplar, of which the authors have no actual knowledge or experience". This complaint could never have been made of Violet Jacob (author of *Flemington*), exquisite silver-point chronicler of the people of her native Angus, or of Elizabeth Robins whose heart-stirring novel, *The Magnetic North*, was based on her own early recollections of the Klondyke.

Historical novels were safe, though Maurice Hewlett could be fairly frank in a lush romantic way—"super-heated stuff" was my husband's word for it. Henry Seton Merriman—I can see the row of his blue and gold volumes yet—and Stanley Weyman who took up the historical novel where Charlotte Yonge and Charles Reade left off, and made it live, we read and re-read. I imagine no young person nowadays would think of doing this, overwhelmed as they must be by the ceaseless stream of new books that pour out of the printing presses.

In 1906 the Annual Register had relented a little, remarking that essay-writing is displayed in more than its usual strength, and mentions G. K. Chesterton, E. V. Lucas, Herbert Paul, Andrew Lang and A. C. Benson. I remember reading all these authors and enjoying them. We of my generation liked essays more than is general today. The urbanity of outlook of the essayist seems out of place in the modern world. Essays on topical subjects that are mostly violent, subversive, and controversial, find favour with the glossy magazines, but the kind of quietly literary *jeu d'esprit* that we all enjoyed seems to have disappeared.

In contrast to these uneventful books *The Prisoner of Zenda* and *Rupert of Hentzau* burst upon the late Victorian scene with a thrilling impact. The conception of Ruritania was new and vivid, a fairy-tale edged with danger. The high romantic devotion of the hero to Princess Flavia, and the sinister machinations of Black Michael left us breathless and gasping, and the death of Rudolf Rassendyl brought tears to many a youthful eye. These books opened up a new world of romance and political intrigue in a frontierless country, a new and unexplored *terrain*. In those two books, Anthony Hope showed a pace and tautness of narrative and a power of gripping his readers which he never achieved again. When he tried his hand at books about the contemporary scene he disappointed some of his readers; but I would recommend one or two of them for the well-observed shrewdness and sense of character, notably *The Intrusions of Peggy*, and a curious political novel called *Quisanté* which brings back to me much that is valuable about the time of which I am writing.

It is difficult to choose favourites amongst the books we read. Looking back we never lacked variety, there was no monotony about them. *The Adventures of an Irish R.M.* swam into my ken one hot day when I was sitting in a tent in Egypt near the Pyramids. Someone gave me this book, saying that they doubted whether I should like it as it was mostly about hunting. It took me the shortest possible time to fall under the spell of E. Œ. Somerville and Martin Ross. Their books are now established classics and need no praise from me. I will merely record that I was entranced (and have continued to be entranced ever since) by the authors' edged style and explosive sense of farce. My life has always been enriched by the epic of Mrs. Knox of Aussolas, culminating in the moment when she hurls her silver entrée dishes out of her bedroom window into the peahen's nest, thinking the stables and her house are on fire. My husband also loved these books, and they are part of the memory of happy family evenings when he read them aloud to us. I fear that reading aloud is another pleasure that has gone by the board with the coming of mechanised amusements. This is sad from a family point of view, as there is no bond like shared love for some story read aloud and enjoyed round the fire.

In my family we often say, "Do you remember that Christmas when we first read *The Turn of the Screw*, or those holidays when we discovered *The King with two Faces*?" My husband read his own books to us aloud chapter by chapter as he wrote them, and our children were always given (by me) something to do with their hands, drawing or sewing, for children are fidgety creatures, and are a restless audience if their hands are not occupied.

I should like to urge those who want to understand Edwardian times to read the novels of that date. It was an unselfconscious age, and those who wrote about it were not ashamed to describe a household of servants, plus gardeners and coachman. They did not disguise the fact that they sent their sons to famous public schools. They wrote of quiet Sunday afternoons in London, of going out to tea in a hansom cab, of dinner parties which lasted long, where good food and wine were enjoyed, and where the politics of the day and books and the Academy pictures could be discussed with only occasional flares of disagreement. They also wrote of going to church and of the length and prosiness of sermons, of tea on the lawn under lime trees loud with bees, of drives to picnic in woods surrounding a country house and of wet walks to leave soup and puddings on the deserving poor—in fact they wrote of a vanished world of leisure and privilege where there was always plenty of time and servants provided an unobtrusive background.

All this has an authentic atmosphere which no histories however well documented and detailed can match. I know from experience how hard some of these books are to get—a public library will occasionally yield up one or two of them. There is something a little apologetic and beaten down about the appearance of these books as if they had been carelessly passed from hand to hand, but the strong binding and clear type had usually well withstood the ravages of fifty years.

I always remind myself of the horse belonging to an inebriated butcher, which stopped automatically at every pub. I can no more pass a shelf of second-hand books than that horse could bypass the Crown and Anchor; and although I have never made any find which would excite a bibliophile, I have sometimes come across the old books which I loved in my youth.

I would recommend Rhoda Broughton's *The Waif's Progress*, published at the turn of the century; it has an irony and outspokenness absent from her other books, and must have shocked and surprised her public. Mary Cholmondely's *Red Pottage* was another surprise—not a saccharine story at all, as it opens with a talk between two men about the unfaithful wife of one of them, and a strange pact which ends in the death of the husband. I remember Mary Cholmondely as a dignified grey-haired lady. I dined in her company on the evening when this book came out. Winston

Churchill was another guest, and he was led up to Miss Cholmondely and introduced to her. Silence ensued and he stood with his head thrust forward as our hostess remarked rather nervously, "I don't suppose you have much time for reading novels, Mr. Churchill?" What he answered I did not hear, but Mary Cholmondely and he seemed after this to get on well together. Obviously he had found time to read hers.

A writer whom I do not hear mentioned now but whose prose style I greatly admired, was Elizabeth von Arnim (Countess Russell). After the success of her first book, she assumed the pen name of "The Author of *Elizabeth and her German Garden*", possibly out of respect for the sensibilities of her German in-laws. She could write mordantly, with a brittle painful sort of facetiousness that almost hurts to read. *Fraülein Schmidt and Mr. Anstruther* written in the form of letters, tells the story of a heart that breaks and mends and breaks again. Her sense of the farce of living—"the long fool's errand to the grave"—never relaxes. But her pen was not always dipped in acid. In *Elizabeth in Rügen*, the story of a delightful summer on that once remote and delectable island, she allowed herself an explicit tenderness not found often in her writing:

"How often in these grey autumn days have I turned my face away from the rain on the windows and the mournful mistiness of the November fields . . . to think with a smile of the beauty of that supper. Not that I had beautiful things to eat, for lengthy consultations with the waiter led only to eggs; but they were brought down steep steps to a little nook among the beeches at the water's edge, and this little nook on that particular evening was the loveliest in the world. Enthusiastically did I eat those eggs and murmur 'Earth has not anything to show more fair'—as much, that is, of it as could be made to apply. Nobody could see or hear me down there screened at the sides and back and overhead by beeches, and it is an immense comfort secretly to quote. . . . My table was nearly on a level with the sea. A family of ducks were slowly paddling about in front of me, making little furrows in the quiet water and giving an occasional placid quack. The ducks, the water, the island of Vilm opposite, the Lauterbach jetty half a mile off across a little bay with a crowd of fisher boats moored near it, all were on fire with the same red radiance. The sun was just down, and the sky behind the dark Putbus woods was a marvel of solemn glory. . . . I could hear the fishermen talking over at the jetty, and a child calling on the island, so absolute was the stillness.

"And almost before I knew how beautiful it was, the rosiness faded off the island, lingered a moment longer on the masts of the fisher boats, gathered at last only in the pools among the rushes, died away altogether; the sky paled to green, a few stars looked out faintly, a light twinkled in the solitary house on Vilm, and the waiter came down and asked if he should bring the lamp. . . . To sit there and look out on what Whitman calls the huge and thoughtful night was a comely and sufficient occupation for the best part of me. . . . With an impatience that surprised him I refused the waiter's lamp."

I so well remember an evening in 1908 when Sir Edward Grey spoke warmly to us of a book he had just read, by two unknown Scottish women—the Findlater sisters. He read aloud extracts from it—it was called *Crossriggs*. Some books are a milestone in one's life. This unpretentious novel about a grey Scottish village not far from Edinburgh, was one of these to me. The story is of a valiant spinster, approaching middle age, who works her fingers to the bone for her feckless old father and her widowed sister's brood of hungry children; and it belongs in the category of "homely" or "fireside" stories, I suppose. But it is shot through and through with the keen pure winds of the north. Alex, the heroine is loved by a much younger man, almost a boy—to him she is all poetry and romance, though she sees herself pitilessly as spare and plain. It cannot end happily, and does not. The writing is as astringent and unadorned as are the bare fields she writes of, and as full of comfort:

"They (Alex and Van) passed the plantation beyond the village, turned down the broad road between dipped hedges where the land sloped in the distance to the sea. Here a part of the sidewalk had been laid with shell-gravel, and for a little there was no sound except the slight scrunching of Alex's footsteps on the splintered shells. . . . At last they came within sight of the sea, gleaming grey in the distance, as if light struck on steel. The tender chill spring wind blew towards them, and from the elm trees in the field a bird sang like a soul in bliss."

Books in those days received respectful treatment from reviewers and were not squeezed into two lines of criticism by a host of other claimants to notoriety. There were long critical columns in that most delightful of daily papers, the green *Westminster Gazette*, which arrived always while we were having tea, and was eagerly seized upon to see which of our favourite authors, Conan Doyle or Kipling or H. G. Wells had produced something new.

All in all the novelist of the Edwardian era who most adroitly exposed its follies and turned them to entertaining account was H. G. Wells. No one who is curious about the Edwardian political scene can neglect his perhaps least read masterpiece, *The New Machiavelli*. My husband said of this book that it was the unsparing mirror of certain aspects of Edwardian society. Among the thinly-veiled portraits is an admiring one of A. J. Balfour as Mr. Evesham, and an uncomplimentary one of the Sydney Webbs as Oscar and Altiora Bailey. Wells had a strong objection to political muddle-headedness and one would have thought that Beatrice and Sydney Webb, the arch-planners who thought that an orderly state guided by trained officials would solve all Britain's problems, would have been congenial to him; but that was not how he saw them. It amuses me because as a young woman I used to hear a great deal about the Webbs and their high thinking and low living. One of the Webbs' dinner parties was described to me by my exquisite American aunt Sophie Grey, whose own entertaining was as individual and perfect as were her clothes—"The potatoes," she said, "were actually put on the table and everyone helped themselves; they were not properly scraped and the 'eyes' were left in them."

In *The New Machiavelli* were several malicious thumbnail sketches of our friends in the Liberal party, which did not amuse either of us, as we were fond of them, the fact that we didn't agree with them making no difference to our affection. We saw a great deal of Violet Markham at that time who, though soberly pleased by the Liberal victory of 1906, held the view that friendship should not be spoiled by differences in political beliefs. Some of our Liberal friends did not hold that view, and we saw less of them.

The character of Evesham is drawn with great care by Wells, and a frank admiration tempered with criticism. The hero of the novel, Dick Remington, says:

"I could talk to Evesham with extraordinary freedom and a rare sense of being understood. Other men have to be treated in a special manner; approached through their own mental dialect, flattered by a minute regard for what they had said and done. Evesham was as widely and charitably receptive as any man I have ever met. The common politicians beside him seemed like rows of stuffy little rooms looking out upon the sea." Wells saw faults in Evesham, as for instance when he saw him in the House of Commons "persistent and persuasive and by all my standards wickedly perverse, leaning over the table with those insistent movements of his hand upon it, or swaying forward with a grip upon his coat lapel. . . ."

"One might think at times there was no more of him than a clever man, happily circumstanced, and finding an interest and an occupation in politics, and then came a glimpse of thought, of imagination, like the sight of a soaring eagle through a staircase skylight . . . no other contemporary politician had his quality. . . . He saw and thought widely and deeply; but at times it seemed to me that his greatness stood over and behind the reality of his life, like some splendid servant, thinking his own thoughts, who waits behind a lesser master's chair."

Fairness of judgment was not Wells' strongest point, but he had a mind which played like a searchlight on the shadowy places of the human heart and mind. Wells takes his hero through one disillusioning political experience after another. Having been a Liberal he gets disgusted with that party, turns towards the emerging Labour party, finds little there to admire, and finally joins the Conservatives, whom he quickly begins to find uncongenial too. He finally finishes off his political career by eloping to Italy with a girl who thinks alike with him, deserting his rather dim and pathetic wife, who has in a bewildered way tried to follow him through all his political adventures.

The New Machiavelli is worth study. It has faults, it is too long drawn out, and there is some repetition in it; but there are some first-rate character studies and he acutely analyses mere cleverness and glib generalisations as opposed to profound and cogent thought. He shows up the House of Commons as a place where half-truths, evasions and endless compromises flourish like weeds. He doesn't try to be at all fair, but often his criticisms find their mark.

I can't resist quoting Wells' picture of a dinner party at Harry Cust's (whom he calls Lord Tarvrille):

"It was an occasion made absurd and strange by the odd accident that the house caught fire upstairs while we were dining below. 'It is a man's dinner,' said Tarvrille, when he invited me; 'everything from Evesham and Gane to Williams the author, and Heaven knows what will happen!' I remember that afterwards Tarvrille was accused of having planned the fire to make his dinner a marvel and a memory. It was indeed a wonderful occasion. There were one or two university dons, Lord George Fisher the racing man, Panmure the artist, two or three big city men, Weston Massinghay, and another prominent Liberal whose name I can't remember, the three men Tarvrille had promised, and Esmeer, etc. We began a little coldly with duologues; but the conversation was already becoming general—so far as the long table permitted—when the fire asserted itself.

"It asserted itself at first as a penetrating and emphatic smell of burning rubber—it was caused by the fusing of an electric wire. The reek found its way into a discussion of the Boxer Rising that had sprung up between Evesham and the others at the end of the table. 'Something burning,' said the man next to me.

" 'Something must be burning,' said Panmure.

"Tarvrille hated undignified interruptions. He had a particularly imperturbable butler with a cadaverous sad face and an eye of rigid disapproval. He spoke to this individual over his shoulder. 'Just see, will you,' he said and caught up the pause in the talk to his left. . . .

"We became aware that Tarvrille's butler had returned. 'Beg pardon, m'lord,' he said, 'the house is on fire. Upstairs m'lord, just overhead. No, m'lord, no immediate danger.'

" 'It's all right,' said Tarvrille to the table generally. 'Go on. It's not a general conflagration and the fire brigade won't

VII. Drawing Room at 30 Upper Grosvenor Street, with William Morris wallpaper and chintzes

VIII.   Bedrooms at 30 Upper Grosvenor Street

be five minutes . . .' It was evident that he didn't want his dinner spoiled.

" 'Thompson, champagne, keep it going,' and Thompson marshalled his assistants . . .

"It is all printed in the vividest way as a picture upon my memory, so that were I a painter I think I could give the deep rich browns and warm greys beyond the brightly-lit table, the various distinguished faces interested and keen above the black and white evening dress, the alert men servants indistinctly seen in the dimness beyond. . . . We seemed to be a little transitory circle in a universe of darkness and violence; an effect to which the diminishing smell of burning rubber, the trampling of feet overhead, the swish of water added enormously.

"Then for a time things became preposterous. There was a sudden cascade of water by the fireplace, and then absurdly the ceiling began to rain on us, first at this point and then at all. 'My new suit!' cried someone. Now a vertical line of blackened water would establish itself and form a spreading pool upon the gleaming cloth.

" 'Draw up,' said Tarvrille, 'that's the bad end of the table.' He turned to the imperturbable butler, 'Take round bath towels,' he said, and presently the men behind us were offering with inflexible dignity, 'Port wine, sir, bath towel, sir?' "

S HOPPING in 1966 is hardly any longer a pleasure. The shops are crowded, the assistants perfunctory and indifferent to their customers. The personal relationship between shopper and saleswoman has gone with so much else, except possibly in some exclusive fashion houses in London or Paris.

My mother and aunts had special friends in the different shops they patronised. At the lace counter in Marshall & Snelgrove, I remember Miss M., who wore a grey false fringe. My aunt, Mrs. Firebrace, liked her very much and after years of buying lace and, I think, handkerchiefs, and exchanging stately conversation, Miss M. was invited to spend the day at the Firebraces' house in Sussex, where she and my aunt had a most pleasing time discussing all sorts of matters in a lovely garden.

This personal service in the shops made one often (I must admit) buy things that were not strictly necessary. It was tempting to go into a shop and get a trifle for oneself (or family) just to feel welcomed and appreciated, and to be absorbed into their lamplit cosiness and carpeted ease on a wet dark November afternoon.

Hugh Walpole put into one of his books a scene in which a bishop's wife buys a hot water bottle at the Army and Navy Stores. One of my cousins remarked that she was glad Hugh Walpole had included this "period" piece into his novel: I remember being surprised, for it never occurred to me that everything would not go on just the same, and I saw in my mind's eye bishops' wives going on and on for decades doing just this. My uncle, Lord Ebury, was Chairman of the Stores; he was succeeded by his youngest son, Francis Ebury, and our family regarded this shop with a special affection, although we reaped no material advantage from our relationship. But when we entered its portals we felt that we belonged there.

Who, able to look back on the Army and Navy Stores of sixty years ago, does not recall with nostalgia the thrilling smell of the Ironmongery Department, which dealt in "Gasfittings, Lamps, Turnery, Brushes, Combs, Baskets, Cooperage, Leathers, Sponges, Oriental Goods, Garden Implements, Barrack Furniture (Sale or Hire), Saddlery, Horse Appointments, Waterproof Goods, etc."

What was the distinguishing characteristic of Barrack Furniture, as distinct from any other kind of furniture? Was it made of wickerwork suitable for sipping sundowners on a verandah? The Stores never let us forget that it had branches in Bombay and Calcutta and this, perhaps, explained the presence of Oriental Goods among the Turnery and Cooperage. The arrangement of the departments too, was extraordinary—why were stamps sold with pianos, and coal and oil with mineral waters?

The Stores issued a book of Order Forms on which you were supposed to enter your monthly or quarterly orders for sugar, tea, soap—(a great many varieties of the latter, Yellow Laundry, Brown Mottled, Brown Windsor, Pears' Transparent, Wright's Coal Tar!).

I sat every week at a table in our house in Hyde Park Square, or later in 13 Bryanston Street, with a pile of invoices impaled on a sharp spike, trying to match them up with a complicated system of numerals in another little brown book issued by "The Stores". The invoices had fish scales adhering to them, also traces of the meat which had been purchased, and this "doing the house books", as it was then called, filled me with distaste. But that was how we did things in those remote days.

When I married, our income was small so I and my friends discussed a great deal where commodities could be got at better prices than the shops we usually dealt with. This led sometimes to absurd results—I was told by someone that it was a good idea to go to a street market in Soho to buy vegetables cheap. I triumphantly purchased two large cauliflowers and being in a hurry took a taxi home, thus wiping out any possible advantage in the way of cheaper vegetables that I had gained.

To revert to the house books, they were the bugbear of many people. Why had we spent more in one week than another? We racked our brains as to whether we had any visitors to lunch or dinner. Less conscientious mistresses of houses left the books undone or in the hands of their cooks, hating the time-consuming boredom of this chore; but those of us who had to watch carefully what money we spent, settled down to the tedious task.

The publishers of Letts Diaries produced a horrid yellow notebook called *Can I Afford It?*, in which you were supposed to keep strict weekly accounts and carry over the balance, if any, in your favour to meet next week's expenses.

For the majority of women the money saved on household expenditure was all they had to spend on themselves—the first thought when economy was inevitable was "cutting down on the books".

Shopping for clothes or household furnishing was a different and much more delightful occupation. If I am to compare then and now, I can only say that the shops carried enormous stocks, and if the shopper wished for a length of material, great bales of merchandise were brought out and displayed, even if one needed only a yard or two. Now, though glittering with fluorescent lighting and embellished

IX.   'Out of a Bandbox'—Alice Grosvenor

X.   Edwardian Hats

with glass and plastic decorations, shops have comparatively small stocks behind their sophisticated façades. It is very often impossible to get some quite simple thing, like a pair of gloves or a jumper, in the size and colour you want; you must take what is there or go elsewhere, only to be told the same story there.

Two wars have spoilt the quality of dress materials and other commodities. After the shortages of 1914 they were never so lavish again. The shopping scene has changed very much. We have caught from America, the pioneers of mass production of cheap and pretty clothes, a transatlantic love of changing the outlines and colour of what we wear, and we discard them quickly in order to look different each month of each year.

In Victorian and even Edwardian times women shopped with enormous care, and often a dress had to last for many years, and be handed down with alterations to a daughter. Someone said of a dress produced in Paris by Worth, "Ce n'est pas une robe c'est un meuble", and lovers of Edith Wharton's novels will remember the two New York ladies who bought their dresses from this famous house, and kept them for a year in their wardrobes before wearing them, so as not to appear vulgarly smart.

When I look through my scrapbooks and at photographs of my old dresses I marvel how we put up with the inconvenience of the clothes we wore. Huge hats pinned on with hat pins over our fluffled-out coiffures, reared up on our heads in a high wind, our long cumbersome skirts with the stiff underskirts picked up mud and grit from pavements and roads. When we clambered into a hansom cab we had somehow to keep our skirts from touching its high muddy wheel—no easy task. We wore feather boas which streamed in every direction, becoming uncurled and damp in rain. We meekly put up with all this, never questioning our absurd bondage. Yet the clothes were pretty and enhancing to those women who knew how to wear them with real elegance. "She looks as if she had stepped out of a bandbox" was the slightly obscure saying then—which means, I suppose, that she had a sort of newly-minted look only produced by the ministrations of a good (often French) maid who knew how to pack.

In Max Beerbohm's *Zuleika Dobson* the mountainous luggage which accompanied an Edwardian beauty on her visits is described:

"The sun streamed through the bay-window . . . and . . . invaded the many trunks which gaped in various stages of excavation around the room. The doors of the huge wardrobe stood, like the doors of Janus' temple in time of war, majestically open; and the sun seized this opportunity of exploring the mahogany recesses.

"But the carpet . . . was now almost hidden from him, hidden under layers of fair fine linen, layers of silk, brocade, satin, chiffon, muslin. All the colours of the rainbow, materialised by modistes, were there. Stacked on chairs were I know not what of sachets, glove cases, fan cases. There were innumerable packages in silver-paper and pink ribands. There was a pyramid of band-boxes. There was a virgin forest of boot-trees.

"And rustling quickly hither and thither, in and out of this profusion, with armfuls of finery, was an obviously French maid. Alert, unerring, like a swallow she dipped and darted. Nothing escaped her, and she never rested. She had the air of a born unpacker—swift and firm, yet withal tender. Scarce had her arms been laden but their loads were lying lightly between shelves or tightly in drawers. To calculate, catch, and distribute, seemed in her but a single process. She was one of those who are born to make chaos cosmic."

"A lady's luggage should look as if it contained at least

two changes" was an Edwardian axiom. What would they say of us with our few possessions stuffed into an overnight bag!

Much has been written on the subject of the spiralling cost of commodities and I shall not add to it; but it amuses me to take a brief look at some old bills which I found in a drawer. One is from the fashionable shoe and boot maker in Duke Street. It is for a pair of brogue shoes and two sets of silk shoe laces, and it came to £1 15s. I remember them; the shoes were neat and durable, and I wore them for years. There is another bill of about the same time from Marshall & Snelgrove. It included lengths of ribbon, curtain materials, a child's dress and shoes, six belts, two pairs of kid gloves, several washleather gloves and many other items. The whole bill amounted to thirteen pounds.

The word "shopping" has now a ring of grim utility. It summons up a vision of a queue of patient people carrying heavy bags of food and cartons of washing powder. It evokes no feeling of elegance or joy. When we think of shopping now we see a mental picture of a stout figure with a scarf round her head in a shapeless coat and heavy boots—or of an ageing man either holding a basket away from him as if its contents would bite, or trying to conceal it by hugging it under one arm. In former days no man would have been seen dead with such a repellent object as a bag of groceries. They might have carried a box of chocolates or a bouquet of flowers to their lady-love, but there they drew the line.

In the days I write of, the word "shopping" had a frivolous connotation, it meant going to buy something pretty (never a household necessity) and if possible completely unnecessary, which was much more fun.

Some ladies were a little furtive about this and were inclined not to mention it in front of their husbands, who might ask awkward questions about how much of their housekeeping money would be spent (or squandered) in shops. Husbands had a way of saying, "Surely, my dear, you don't need a new dress, the one you have had for three years still looks very nice", or "the drawing-room curtains look all right to me, my mother never bought new curtains and she was married for fifty years." But no remarks like this ever diverted a hardened shopper from her goal.

Mothers had a different technique. When they did not wish to buy something their daughters wanted, they would say, "We will think about it, dears, after all it won't run away."

A visit to Paris meant for people who were not rich a glorious adventure of gazing and fingering. This very often resulted only in the purchase of a hat at the Bon Marché or the Magasin du Louvre, then blessedly cheap and alluring. The hat was apt to be a little too avant-garde in fashion to go well with one's London clothes, but it was a Paris hat and that was that.

We had a touching faith in what clothes could do to help our looks. "If only," a penniless woman would exclaim, "I could afford really good clothes instead of going to little dressmakers and buying 'reach me downs' in shops."

We must have bought literally miles of the kind of beaded trimmings called *passementerie* with which to renovate ageing dresses. And we always seemed to have broken fans to be repaired. They were repaired by Duvelleroy in Bond Street, which sold nothing else but fans and apparently throve on their sales. We held them in our hands when we went to dinners and dances. They were charming fragile objects made of lace sprinkled with sequins, mounted on mother-of-pearl sticks. If they slipped through our hands on to the floor they broke, and a clumsy partner at a dance could smash a stick as he handed one's fan.

A kind friend of ours, Sir Lionel Phillips, presented me

with a huge ostrich feather fan. I loved this fan, and held it in front of me, fanning myself so vigorously that an elderly lady sitting next to me complained of the draught it made.

Fans now are out of fashion, and so is the hand-made lace, which was kept folded away in blue tissue paper in cardboard boxes. Will it ever be used again? So much in fashion goes, but also it returns! Real lace can be lovely to wear, enhancing the wearer as no machine-made imitation can.

My mother liked the shops which she had always known, and we shopped mostly at Marshall & Snelgrove, Harvey Nichols, Gorringe's, and Woolland's. She felt safe there, she was known to the assistants, they stocked her requirements.

To the younger people the shops were just shops and we didn't enquire into their beginnings. But now a very interesting book has come out.* In it we are told that for instance, Gorringe started in a small way in 1858, that Debenham & Freebody's suddenly enlarged itself in 1907 by completing a handsome new building, and issued a souvenir booklet which held out the attraction that you could get lunch or tea at moderate charges in a quiet elegant restaurant—a great innovation indeed!

Marshall & Snelgrove had had its moment of high romance. We were told with bated breath by our mother and aunts how Lady Florence Paget, daughter of Lord Anglesey, went one day with her fiancé, Mr. Henry Chaplin, to inspect part of her trousseau there. She left him waiting outside the Oxford Street entrance, ran through the shop and out by the door into Henrietta Street, where she met Lord Hastings whom she married later in the day. History does not relate how long Henry Chaplin waited for her, or what he said when she did not return to his side. (The next time he met her she was the Marchioness of Hastings.) This story gave London society much to talk about

* *Shops and Shopping*, by Alison Alburgham.

and made Marshall & Snelgrove a place of great interest to lady shoppers, especially those who were young and romantically inclined.

The Edwardian lady in retrospect had the destructible fragility of a hybrid tea-rose. One thinks of her surrounded by appurtenances that were necessities then, though they would be considered just dust-catching now—heavy cut-glass scent-bottles, with gilt stoppers, tortoise-shell-backed hair-brushes—sitting in a swansdown-trimmed dressing jacket, in a bedroom decked with pale fresh chintzes and spotted muslin flounces, with ribbon-embroidered cosies for the hotwater cans on the marble-topped washstand.

Edith Wharton writing in 1905 drew in Lily Bart a girl who was the quintessence of this sort of helpless fragility and elegance: "Her maid had kindled a little fire on the hearth, and it contended cheerfully with the sunlight which slanted across the moss-green carpet and caressed the curved sides of an old marquetry desk. Near the bed stood a table holding her breakfast tray, with its harmonious porcelain and silver, a handful of violets in a slender glass, and the morning paper folded beneath her letters. There was nothing new to Lily in these tokens of a studied luxury. . . ."

After Lily's death in poverty Lawrence Selden looks round the lodging house bedroom in which she lies: "There was very little furniture in the room. The shabby chest of drawers was spread with a lace cover and set out with a few gold-topped boxes and bottles, a rose-coloured pincushion, a glass tray strewn with tortoise-shell hair pins—he shrank from the poignant intimacy of these trifles. . . ."

I can recall a party to which I was taken by an aunt when I was just grown up and painfully shy. Georgina Lady Dudley sat on a sofa near the fire looking magnificently beautiful. We had been (like the less worthy females in Jane Austen's novels) invited to come in after dinner. A young man played Brahms, and our hostess's daughter, who was piquant-looking but no beauty, wore a wreath of life-sized pale blue and white convolvulus flowers round her head. I wished, as often before, that the solid parquet floor would open and swallow my dowdiness.

The beauties of my youth had a sort of serenity like goddesses, even if it was sometimes the serenity which sprang from arrogance. They expected to be stared at, and they were.

VIRGINIA WOOLF once said to me that she pitied the children of today who lived in flats, and who had never lived in houses with dark corners or with long ill-lighted passages to shudder at. She also said that they had none of the delicious sense of enjoyment which we had when we inserted ourselves through the green baize door, which sealed the rest of the house from the kitchen quarters, where a vivid and individual life went on.

Children's relationships with family servants varied a great deal. There was an element of cupboard-love toward the cook, whose temper was uncertain (the lick of a spoonful of treacle, or a sweetmeat filched from the edge of a wire tray, had to be accomplished by stealth). One always had to be wary of cooks, whose legs from endless standing were apt to bother them, and who, from bending over saucepans, grew flushed and breathless. They were apt to dismiss one with, "Now run along. I've got my work to do."

Butlers were kinder, and we would sometimes be allowed to help in the ritual of polishing the silver; housemaids were a little apt to make remarks about the way we had kicked the paint on their staircase when our boots were muddy, and spilt paint water on a bedroom carpet.

But on the whole the atmosphere behind the baize door was one of jokes and laughter, and from a child's point of view far preferable to that of the drawing-room where we found it only too easy to knock something over. We viewed our mother's lady visitors with distaste, as we knew very well that as they drove home they would say to each other something like "Norman's and Caroline's girls are (1) rather boisterous (2) spoilt, (3) not so attractive as we should have supposed"—we had overheard remarks like these.

The children who penetrated behind the baize door often came to know a great deal more of what was going on in the house than their parents ever imagined. To us the vivid and interesting life going on below stairs was like the difference between eating plain bread and a rich cake.

I possess a book by Lady Jekyll with the unpretentious title of *Kitchen Essays, with recipes and their occasions*. This book was not published till 1922, but it has an Edwardian flavour. Post-war shortages after 1918 are mentioned but not stressed, and one marvels at the lavishness of the materials the writer regards as necessities.

There is a story that one of the Rothschilds was heard to remark that a good dish could be made by first taking the roes of nine hen lobsters. Lady Jekyll indulges in no such regal fantasies, but she does suggest that to make good orange jelly you should start by obtaining eighteen oranges.

She was noted for the excellence of the meals served in her house, also for her intimate knowledge of cooking and her practical common sense. The essays range over many subjects and are garnished with apt quotations in prose and poetry to give them a literary turn; but as one turns her pages it is obvious that she understood everything possible about entertaining in the best and most sensible way.

The only exception to this seems to me her chapter on "When the cook is away", where she supposes that the kitchenmaid can be persuaded to attempt *Lobster à la Lyonnaise*, Orange Jumbles and *Bifteck à la Russe*. She ends this chapter with the words, "Leaving these instructions (*i.e.* as to how these complicated viands are to be made) before your kitchen maid's eyes, the sound of your stimulating words of hope and faith in her ears, you will be able to transfer the burden on to her shoulders, and go up and dress for dinner feeling that you have done your duty." Lady Jekyll must certainly have known a paragon of a kitchen maid!

She throws a revealing light on how a life lived in a highly civilised era should be conducted. She begins with "*Le mot juste* in food". She goes on to a chapter called "Men Only". She has a high opinion of bachelor entertaining and considers that they are better at ordering a dinner from a chef than their female counterparts.

Lady Jekyll also considers that the master of the house is better at coping with domestic upsets, and she relates a pleasant story of a country house in a remote district, filled to overflowing by guests and family, when the entire kitchen staff threatened to leave. "Shortage of water, conflicting milk claims by rival nurseries, etc., had produced a disaster imminent and irretrievable. 'But what did you say to them all?' asked a trembling and defeated mistress of the house when her husband returned from the back regions. 'If you are a sensible woman, and I know you are, you will never ask or try to find out,' was the enigmatic reply. But anyhow the barometer was set fair, and the dinner that night specially successful. Was it flattery? Was it *largesse*? Was it that combination of a square jaw and a twinkling eye which is often so persuasive? No one will ever know, but the kitchen was a place of sunshine and the cook even volunteered to write out four recipes of her best efforts for an appreciative guest."

For breakfast there would have been poached, boiled and scrambled eggs, haddock, kidneys, hot rolls, three kinds of marmalade and a "cold table" of ham, and cold grouse. No cartons of cornflakes on the table would have been permitted.

Lady Jekyll sweeps masterfully on with directions for "A dinner before the play", "A little supper after the play",

"A shooting party luncheon", "Luncheon for a motor excursion in winter", "Cottage hospitality" (including a *potage maigre* and a bread and butter pudding), "Tray food" (for invalids), "Dance and supper dishes", "Food for artists and speakers", which includes light dishes for before and after speeches. Two chapters which cater "For the too thin" and "the too fat" are full of wise advice. Then follow "Sunday suppers", "Wedding breakfasts", "Their first dinner party", "Meat-less meals", "Food for the punctual and unpunctual", "Hints for holiday housekeeping", and so on, covering a way of life now irretrievably gone. (She doesn't mention funeral bakemeats, but otherwise every other activity seems to be catered for.)

The reader is struck by the amount of hard work and intelligence which was put into cooking. One is also amazed by the amount of kitchen and pantry washing-up which would have been necessary in carrying out any of Lady Jekyll's instructions in this book. In case one of my readers would like to attempt one of Lady Jekyll's recipes, here it is. It is for a Viennese *Torte* for a siren's party of two. "Clarify 1 lb butter. When cold beat to a cream, add 12 ozs of sugar, 1 lb potato flour (sieved). Beat the whole mass for one hour, when it should form bubbles. Bake in a bread-crumbed mould in a moderate oven."

We are apt to envy past times, a barren activity to my mind. But if one does permit oneself to sigh a little it should be for the size of Edwardian appetites, and their ability to gratify them.

ONCE when I was living in London in my youth I remarked to an aunt of mine how much I wished I had a garden of my own. She replied, "It is wiser to keep a garden as a plum for your middle age". In her opinion gardening was a treat for the not so young.

In these starker years I have looked back sometimes with envy to those Edwardian ladies who called themselves "great gardeners"; they had all the enjoyment and none of the hard work we have. They had the palm without the dust, in other words they had little or no acquaintance with pests and weeds.

The aunt in question had an exquisite garden in Sussex, and so little was she encouraged to work in it by her admirable gardener, that she concentrated all her attention on a small wood with a pond in its centre which adjoined her property. She indulged her fancy of growing foxgloves and other woodland flowers round the pond, and she removed every twig as soon as it fell from one of the trees. She gave it the rather quaint look of an outdoor boudoir, so neat and smooth it was. It held an enormous fascination for children, this neat little wood with its dark pool in the centre, but it was a mother's nightmare, because any deviation in the pattern was remarked and at once censured.

The Edwardian era saw the beginning of gardens that had personality. The Sussex gardener, Mr. Robinson, with Miss Gertrude Jekyll* and others, invented and promoted the massed effects of the herbaceous border and helped to free

* Sister-in-law of Lady Jekyll

the garden from its Victorian strait-jacket. The Victorians had been fond of flower "beds", that from a distance looked like a mosaic of crude colours. Flower-beds were often crescent or star shaped and contained a rather bizarre succession of plants. One of their favourites, a plant with fleshy grey leaves and waxy pink flowers, I have seen arranged in curved arabesques the whole length of a flower border. Between these curves were small tight clumps of blue lobelias varied by pale yellow calceolarias interspersed with pink geraniums and scarlet verbenas. Geraniums proliferated in stone urns and occasionally there would be a bed of heavenly smelling heliotrope. The general effect of a bedded-out garden was stylised and to our way of thinking, ugly.

A bedded-out garden strikes us latter-day gardeners with awe, as we know the hard work entailed to ensure an unvarying succession of plants, drilled to bloom at the same time. Our taste in gardens has so radically changed that we marvel that this cast-iron perfection and regularity can ever have given pleasure.

It gave place to the Edwardian taste for massed effects in long borders which were, indeed, at their best, a succession of loveliness. The garden was no longer entirely a gardener's garden. The lady of the house began to indulge her taste in colour and her preferences in scent. Her hands were stoutly gloved for the tying up of roses and she wore a wide gardening hat which could be pretty or ugly according to the taste of the wearer. Very often it was pretty because the ladies of that epoch did not care to look plain. But it was always shady, as sunburn and freckles were not considered as aids to beauty. A chiffon veil was sometimes tied over the hat and under the chin.

Miss Jekyll writes: "Conifers were crowded into every garden as exponents of the horticultural tastes of the day, happily our gardens are no longer peppered with conifers."

Shrubberies were beloved of children as affording hideouts for games of hide-and-seek, but were mostly abolished by the Edwardians in all but gardens of large houses which had parks around them which stretched behind and around formal terraces.

"In the Edwardian garden any trees had to be severely pruned and at the same time thrown into carefully considered groups," Miss Jekyll comments. She continues, "The border has a different colour scheme; at the two ends blue, white and palest yellow with grey foliage or purple, white and pink, also with grey foliage respectively. The colour then advancing from both ends by yellow and orange to the middle glory of the strongest reds at both ends."

Often a flight of steps had aubretia and alyssum cascading down on each side with tall flowers like foxgloves filling in at the back. Gardens were planned to be a part of life. As soon as one stepped out of the house one could choose a background to suit one's mood. Seats were placed in all sorts of corners from which there was a view through trees of the surrounding countryside, or a vista along a pleached alley or a pergola. Pergolas with roses climbing all over them cropped up in most gardens. Leisure and pleasure were the keynotes of the Edwardian garden—and to many people sitting on a garden seat the view from it meant little. A garden was a place where conversation could be carried on in greater privacy than in the house in which they were staying—and I remember many long talks with the young man of the moment, or another girl, in a background of scented flowers haunted by bees and butterflies.

There was usually a small lily pond by which one could sit, surrounded by tall spiky plants where the flash of a goldfish's tail could be seen among the flat water-lily leaves.

One of the gardens where I spent much time in my youth

was Levens Hall in Westmorland. It had beautiful old horn-beam hedges in front of which were planted red and orange flowers. This was a garden made for conversation and dreaming—an enchanted place where one could while away the time with or without a book. The ancient house built round a pale tower encouraged musing on the past, and the sight of our hostess in her flowing dress and large garden hat wandering about gathering flowers added to the quiet charm of this enchanted place.

The Edwardian possessor of a garden often had admirable taste, and was in the happy position of having as her coadjutor a head gardener with possibly an under-gardener and a useful satellite called "the gardener's boy", who dug, weeded and swept up leaves, tidied the paths, dug moss out of paving-stones and generally attended to everything that no one else wanted to do. The head gardener was usually an expert at his job and his relationship with the lady of the garden varied from the affection which springs up between two people who have the same end in view, to the secret wish that she would take herself off to her duties in the house, and not interfere or criticise his own labours.

The head gardener of yesterday (and I have known many) was the sworn foe of children, whose small but sturdy feet could trample on delicate plants and who were apt to bowl a hoop through a clump of carefully grown flowers. Some head gardeners did not in their heart of hearts like anyone to pick the flowers except themselves. They were usually dour, independent men, dressed in the oldest of clothes with cloth caps on their heads which they did not see fit to remove. They knew all about greenhouses, and the treatment of espaliered fruit. They easily obtained ample stores of manure and had a first-rate working knowledge of different soils. They knew also every clump of flowers intimately, and no plant could be surreptitiously slipped into a border without raising a respectful but critical comment. A compromise was usually arrived at by the lady of the garden keeping a small part of it for her own cultivation into which she stuck plants which she had acquired by gift or purchase. The gardener watched the progress of these plants with sardonic amusement and would offer no advice on their culture unless directly asked to do so. It often ended in their being given over to him to transplant into his own domain, where they rapidly improved and flourished under his expert care, and the lady was left in no doubt as to his thoughts, even though he did not permit himself to express them in words.

The ladies wisely turned to easier avocations, such as dead-heading the roses, and I well remember seeing one of my aunts, wearing long white gloves and kneeling on a mat, patiently snipping off the withered heads of the Mrs. Simpkins pinks—a very rewarding task as the pinks kept on blooming all the summer long, looking like an exquisite white velvet ribbon looped around her rose beds.

The Edwardian garden yielded a profusion of flowers for the house which were not arranged with the skill and care of today. In most country houses there was somewhere a small room called the Flower Room into which they were brought heaped up in flat baskets. They were apt to be crammed into vases. Flowers were—well, flowers, and their beauty was supposed to speak for itself.

Many of the richer Edwardians preferred flowers grown in the greenhouses and frames to decorate their drawing-rooms. Malmaison carnations, frilly and heavily scented, *La France* roses, Parma violets, stephanotis and gardenias stood about in gilt baskets and jardinières.

My aunt who snipped the white pinks, unlike many of her friends, loved wild flowers, and one day she went to a nearby field and brought back an armful of buttercups. She arranged them in tall china vases on her mantelpiece. A rich and important cousin came to see her, and she never forgot the contemptuous glance he gave her, though he made no comment on the buttercups. It was quite obvious to her that their bright and delicate beauty meant nothing to him, and that he was amazed that she had failed to decorate her mantelpiece with some flowers more suitable for a lady's drawing-room.

What the late Victorians and Edwardians would think of our carefully arranged red cabbage leaves, silvered teazles, and dried beech leaves, or of the Cape gooseberries which sparsely decorate so many contemporary rooms in the winter, I can only too well imagine.

So much that is important and vital has gone in the two wars which have torn down the fabric of our lives, that it is perhaps absurd to drop a tear for the loss of the lavish Edwardian garden with its acres of ribbon-mown lawns. I will confine myself to a mild regret that to most of us the garden is no longer a place where we can have any peace.

I remember so many golden afternoons which slipped away while one read or daydreamed. Now to most of us this would be impossible. Gardening is a battle, and a truceless one. Never can we take a chair out on a fine afternoon without our conscience (that nagging nuisance) saying *sotto voce*, "Just look at the weeds. You ought to do something about them. The ground elder is going to strangle the irises. That straggling bush must be pruned. Those polyanthus are crying out to be divided. You must get your gardening fork and secateurs, and work and work"—and even if you try to still the voice of conscience the discomfort remains in your mind. You find yourself rising from your chair and going angrily in search of your gardening tools; your books, embroidery and writing materials lying discarded on the grass.

But there are moments of compensation for all the sense of loss. Gone the hard-edged perfection. Gardens now have

75

much beauty and the ranges of flowering shrubs which are replacing the herbaceous border have their own charm, The sun shines and the birds sing, and the wind chases the shadows of the leaves to and fro across the lawn, and lo and behold, there is a flower which one has grown oneself from seed, or a cutting which has successfully struck, or a sickly bush which under constant care has now produced two sizeable roses.

THE contrasts in the life of the poor and of those who were wealthy or comfortably off were very great. On the one hand there was by our standards extraordinarily comfortable living, and on the other the direst squalor and degradation.

The situation is set out with dispassionate clarity in *Edwardian England* and it is a saddening indictment of the time. How, we ask now, could so many people have lived so comfortably without any pricks of conscience? The answer is that most better-off Edwardians had very little actual contact with poverty. If business took them through slum districts they averted their heads, and tried to forget what they had seen. They may have had the Bible in their minds which says that the poor will always be with us. It was still the London of Dickens; much of it was still the London of Hogarth and Dr. Johnson.

Beggars lurked in doorways or stood outside shops, theatres and churches, and a drive through the poorer parts of London showed children in rags and shoeless, and other disquieting features, such as broken windows stuffed up with old newspapers, gutters choked with refuse and crowded tenements in dark disease-breeding alleys.

"Owing to the dietary deficiencies imposed by ignorance the differences between the physical conditions of rich and poor were gross, as a few statistics show. The average height of working-class school-boys was five inches below that of the public school, and the average weight of working-class school-boys was eleven pounds less than that of the boys from wealthier families. At the beginning of the period, 18 per cent of children born in the west end of London died before the age of five: in the east-end 55 per cent did so . . . in Blackburn, for instance, 1911, the infantile death rate in the wealthier area was 26 per 1,000, in the poorer areas 315 per 1,000."*

The housing of the poor was scandalously bad. In poorer districts many houses all over the kingdom were without water taps or any form of sanitary accommodation. A typical description of such conditions comes first from Doctor Alfred Salter when he visited a maternity case in Bermondsey at the turn of the century: "It was a cold day, but the family was so poor that they had not even a penny to put into the meter for heat. The house was one up, one down, with a small scullery and no backyard, for drying and washing were done in the front court where there was one stand-pipe with water for twenty-five houses, with the water on for two hours daily—though never on Sundays. . . . There was one water closet for the twenty-five houses and a cesspool. Queues lined up outside that water closet, men, women and children, every morning before they went to work. . . . There was no possibility of decency or modesty or health for these people. . . . The conditions of thousands of homes were the same."†

I am, however, not attempting to write a treatise on the conditions of England, and am only trying to illuminate the subject by a few personal memories. To those of us who had an awareness of poverty and a strong desire to help the picture was bewildering. The legacy of the Industrial Revolution seemed, as far as the poorer classes were concerned, to be an Augean stable, and it appeared to many of us that it was only possible, in spite of all our well-meant efforts, to sweep round its edges.

* *Edwardian England*, p. 205.   † *Edwardian England*, p. 156.

The churches of all denominations strove manfully to help, and charitable societies abounded. It is customary now to speak slightingly of them, but they gave useful care to men out of work, to old people and children. Some of them, it is true, were badly managed and were thinking in outdated terms of Victorian philanthropy, but they did help those who sorely needed help.

I soon got bored with the idleness of my life as a young lady, and my father having been a friend of Sir Charles Loch, I offered my services to the small branch of the Charity Organisation Society (of which Sir Charles Loch was the founder) in Baker Street. It was a very small office. Letters were handwritten, and there was little office equipment; but the filing system was good, and the work done was systematic and thorough. The C.O.S. was then a highly controversial activity. Its aims were to work hand-in-hand with local authorities, and to try to cut at the roots of poverty by first trying to see its problems as a whole. I don't imagine that I can have helped them much, as I worked as a kind of dog's body licking envelopes in this office, but I gratefully acknowledge how much good they did to *me*. I was promoted to looking through their files and I was instructed in one of their firmest tenets—which was that no case which came to be helped should ever be closed until *Finis* could be written on it.

As I have said, beggars abounded in the streets, and rich passers-by would be blackmailed into handing out money, as a salve to their consciences. We were taught by the C.O.S. never to do this, as many of the beggars were skilled in preying on the guilty feelings of richer people. If, the C.O.S. sternly said, you are sorry for these people in the streets, you must talk to them and enter into their problems, and try and get them jobs, or help them with their children: but you must never shovel out money and walk rapidly away. By doing this you are making bad things worse.

There was another branch of our activities. The writing of begging letters had become a flourishing industry, and the C.O.S. probed deeply into these. It was my job to read many of them; they were heart-rending and nearly reduced me to tears. But seen in the cold light of research they were almost always spurious. More and more people sent the begging letters they received to the C.O.S. to investigate. (Begging letters were not a novelty belonging only to this era. The Iron Duke received many of them, and sent money for years to needy families who existed only on paper.)

The C.O.S. was unpopular in some quarters. It is curious that now when everyone spends a large part of their lives answering questions about their most intimate affairs and filling up forms and generally suffering from a lack of privacy, that poor people of those days often refused to go and seek help from the C.O.S. because they did not wish to be questioned about their circumstances. Herbert Woollcombe, one of the officials of the C.O.S. and a fine and dedicated man, gave a lecture to some working-men's club on the poems of Tennyson. At the end of his talk a man rose in the audience remarking with emphasis that he didn't care two-pence about Tennyson, but that he thought the Charity Organisation Society should be swept from the face of the earth.

In spite of criticisms the C.O.S. continued to flourish, and to do excellent work in all areas of social welfare. Many activities which are common form today, and which are now sponsored and run by the Greater London Council were originated by it.

I had the great good fortune to have Violet Markham as a friend. She was wealthy and finely generous with her money, and cared intensely for helping people in the most constructive possible way. She came from a family of coal magnates in Chesterfield and her educational settlement in that town was a model. She was hard-headed and unsentimental in her approach to life, while generous to everyone who needed help from her—preferring generally to remain anonymous.

I helped her to start the Personal Service League. It stemmed from a sermon by Canon Hensley Henson on conditions among the poor, and a group of people who heard him preach agreed to appeal for helpers who would each look after several needy families. In practice we found that this kind of work was not really constructive and could only be of slight use. The Personal Service League developed as a society for studying the problems of poverty and unemployment. Each member of it took a practical course in, say, work with a Care Committee, and attended lectures on the structure of local government.

I can remember reading William Beveridge's book *Unemployment* and being deeply interested in the start of the Labour Exchanges. At a dinner party I was introduced to a young man, a Mr. Beveridge. I eagerly said how pleased I was to meet him. He replied, "But you know I am not the golfer?" I laughed. I have always had a mild horror of any game, and I explained that it was Labour Exchanges and not golf which interested me.

There have been countless serious books written about poverty in Edwardian days. Research of all kinds has been done, facts, figures and statistics have been compiled, which are there for anyone to read and mark. But nothing can compare with the impact made on the mind of a book by a fine writer who describes with clarity and compassion poverty seen at first hand.

Among many books I would choose two for their sincerity and beauty. Flora Thompson's *Lark Rise to Candleford* is now in The World Classics, and set for G.C.E. examinations. We claim it as our Oxfordshire classic, as she lived just within the limits of our county in a hamlet too small to have a church or school. Her record starts in late Victorian times and carries on into this century. It describes the starkest kind of rural poverty. There is no trace of self-pity, no envy of richer people, in Laura, who is the heroine of the book and is a portrait of Flora Thompson herself. It is a most unusual book because the writer has an unflinching eye for life and the human situation. But she also has a poet's feeling for this bit of English countryside, and describes the flat fields and their waving corn with an artist's eye, so that while her books are a mine of information for students of social history, they are also a delight to those who love beautiful and sensitive descriptions of a beloved countryside.

The other book I would like to mention is *The Poor Man's House* written by Stephen Reynolds and published in 1908. It deals with poverty from a very different angle to that of Flora Thompson, for Stephen Reynolds came from a middle-class background and would be called a Socialist now. He went to live in a seaside town in Devon in a fishing slum and embraced poverty with idealistic fervour and enthusiasm. He was anti-bourgeois, anti-State Church education, and especially bitter against anyone who was striving to better the conditions of poverty. He thought such people were interfering and useless, in fact nagging nuisances.

The fisherman and his wife with whom he lived, he describes as splendid human beings and he exalts their home-spun virtues, preferring dirt, smells, lack of sanitation and coarse food to a more refined existence.

The copy I have is a review copy sent by Stephen Reynolds' publishers to my husband, who admired this book very much. He gave it a very favourable review (I think in the *Spectator*), and it certainly has beautiful passages in it—especially those in which the author describes the courage of the fishermen, their fine skills, their uncanny knowledge of the changes of weather, and quotes the cynical remarks they made about the visitors, who with no knowledge of the sea, hired their boats for sea trips in the summer.

This book is social history of a first-hand kind, but not unbiased like *Lark Rise to Candleford* because Stephen Reynolds had intentionally alienated himself from the *milieu* he sprang from. One wonders how economic conditions of today would have appeared to him. I think he would not have wanted to see the fine independence of his fisher people undermined by the Welfare State. This was the attitude of Dickens to the underprivileged of his day. Again and again he exalts the most frugal and self-respecting of his characters, and asks us to admire the fierce pride with which they repudiate our sympathy. But there is no suggestion of altering the *status quo*.

Bad housing was the root cause of infant mortality. During the latter part of the 1914 war, I myself with a group of friends worked steadily in Kentish Town. We were specially interested in clinics for mothers and children. We started and ran a crèche and a nursery school in Gospel Oak Grove. We, and other agencies, by our efforts reduced the infant mortality figures in this district. However, once when talking to a social worker of vast experience I told her rather proudly of what we had achieved, and she said, "No work you do will ever reduce the infant mortality figures below a certain point until housing has been improved," and of course she was right.

The conditions in rural areas often supposed by novelists to be idyllic, were not good. The cottages in villages were dark and damp with tiny windows, and often roofed with mouldering thatch. They depended entirely on the goodwill of their landlord for necessary repairs. There was more food about as vegetables could be grown, hens and a pig could be kept, picking up a living after a fashion. The rural child was also free to roam the fields and woods, and breathe uncontaminated air. It is, however, not uninteresting to note that rural conditions have improved very slowly.

When first we went to live at Elsfield near Oxford in the 1920s, few cottages had inside sanitation, or even an indoor tap for cold water, and the village women had to draw water from a standpipe in the road. These women wore drab clothes of the fashion of a decade earlier, and often an old cloth cap of their husband's; children wore their parents' clothes, cut down. Villages now have mains water and the country-woman's clothes are as pretty and well-chosen as anyone else's, but it took a long time for this to come.

The Edwardian era was not notable for practical or pleasing building; rural houses were poorly designed according to the bad standards of the late Victorians. I remember from visiting the people who lived in them, that they had breakneck staircases, poky kitchens, small windows and seldom faced the right way. Many modern cottages cannot be called pleasing to the eye, but have at any rate at least one big window which allows the inmates to get some sunshine in their rooms.

As I have said, agricultural workers living in tied cottages were completely dependent on their landlord, landowner or farmer as the case might be. Country landlords were often extravagant in their own lives, but callous about the housing of their workers, and sometimes they salved their consciences with presents at Christmas, Harvest Festival suppers and Christmas dinners, while ignoring leaking roofs, crumbling walls and blocked up drains. This was at the worst, but there were many exceptions whose repairs were done promptly and adequately.

Undeserved sneers have been directed at the Lady of the Manor who blandly dispensed soup and blankets, but it must be admitted by any impartial observer that she was often the one who urged her husband on to carry out the work of repairing cottages. Farmers' wives were in my experience totally indifferent as to how their workers lived. The Lady of the Manor should have her place of honour in the history of the countryside.

In many villages today there is no vicarage (if their parish has been joined to another village in which the vicar prefers to live). The school has been closed and the manor-house is either an institution, or lived in by people who have no sense of responsibility to their neighbours, who come from a different world of business or politics, and who may be in residence for only a small part of the year. The old pattern of village life has been broken—and although money is plentiful, because agricultural wages are high, and many village people go out to work daily in some nearby factory, the leadership from the top, from manor and vicarage, has often gone, and there is nothing to take its place.

To revert to Edwardian days. The vicar or rector's wife was an important part of village life. The parson took an active part in the Church school and his wife was supposed to make herself conversant with the situation of every cottager. The vicar took Sunday School but his wife kept the accounts of the Shoe and Coal Clubs, and was expected to hold a weekly work-party (with tea) to which the village women could come and sew for their homes and families—the vicar's wife buying the materials wholesale—thus enabling the workers to get them at a cheaper price than in the shops. Foreign missions neither slumbered nor slept and were always in need of funds. The struggle to raise money was unending.

Vicarages built in the eighteenth or nineteenth centuries were always large and full of draughty passages. Kitchens were stone-flagged and there were wine and coal cellars with stone steps down to them. The rooms were lit with lamps which took at least an hour every day to clean, and they were impossible to keep warm with only one coal-consuming Victorian grate.

The wives of the clergy could seldom afford skilled help and had to make do with a local girl who could scrub and wash and carry coals, but not much else. Trollope's Mr. Crawley, always held up as an example of dire clerical poverty, had a girl from the local orphanage, spoken of as "the red-armed child", from having her arms always plunged in cold water.

All vicarages had large untidy gardens. At the time when they were built, when the living was the portion of the second son of a landed family, labour was cheap and plentiful, and the vicar then had a position to keep up that had nothing to do with his sacred office. Very often there were large roomy stables, as well as a large roomy house, for the parson with sporting tastes. All this had changed by the end of the Edwardian era, but the parson and his wife had to go on keeping up appearances for the sake of the parish and the honour of the Church.

The Lady of the Manor lent her garden for Church fêtes and heroically saw the public trampling down her lawns, or her drawing-room for Church sales, or her dining-room for the Sunday School play.

It was all part of a pattern of country life that seemed then as immutable as the laws of nature.

XI. An Edwardian Lady in her Garden—Constance Lady Wenlock

XII.   A Hansom Cab

MEMORY is rather like a looking-glass whose silver plate time has a little dimmed. You breathe inadvertently on the glass as you go close to look into it and blur the very thing you are trying to re-capture.

The people I write of are those whose outlines have stayed sharp and vivid in my mind. I will speak first of the women, graceful, gifted, or not beautiful but clever and unexpected.

Pamela Glenconner, *née* Wyndham (sister of George Wyndham) comes first into my mind with her pure oval face and delicate features. We stayed with her at the Glen in Peeblesshire when we first married. I arrived blinking rather like an owl in daylight, as we were living with our baby daughter in pleasant but sombre lodgings in Manor Place, Edinburgh. We had been fed on a rather stodgy diet of porridge, "minced collops" and sheeps' tongues, and it was refreshing to come into a house where fruit of all kinds was on the table and where the conversation dwelt on poetry and literature. Pamela Glenconner was delightful to talk to about books. She was uninterested in the ordinary things of life, mince and sheeps' tongues never crossed her mind. The Glen was a house which had been built by her father-in-law, Sir Charles Tennant, in a heavily Scotch baronial style. It looked very out of place in a shallow upland glen, and he was criticised by the Peeblesshire people for not having built a low white-washed house more in keeping with older Peeblesshire houses. But Pamela created her own atmosphere whereever she went. Inside was all light and prettiness, and books were everywhere.

She wrote herself, and made an interesting anthology called *The White Wallet*. Her books were often about Wilsford in Wiltshire, a beautiful place on the downs which her whole family loved. She wrote mostly about the downs and old country sayings and doings. *The White Wallet* is one of those anthologies which are interesting because they show a selective reader's special tastes and are full of quotations of varying merit from now long-forgotten books. Anthologies were then something of a literary innovation.

Pamela always seemed to me an Olympian character, because of her aloofness from mundane things. She floated to and fro between Wilsford and the Glen, appreciating their different beauties, and so well buttressed by wealth that she never had to catch a bus or bother about the price of fish. But even these Olympian people are subject to the hammer blows of fate, and the Glenconners' beloved eldest son was killed in the war—leaving one lovely poem which has been much quoted.

Fortunately her life ended before old age came upon her. After Lord Glenconner died she had married Sir Edward Grey (Lord Grey of Falloden) as his second wife. Her death left him (for the second time in his life) bereaved of a beloved companion to face an old age of near blindness which he bore with striking courage and fortitude. His beautiful head, like that of a Roman poet, is before me as I write these words.

Another friend older than myself, who was neither literary nor particularly handsome, was Sylvia Gleichen (first Countess Gleichen, and then when some foreign royal titles were revised, Lady Edward Gleichen). She came from a gay Irish family and at her house one met diplomats and people from varying worlds, all enjoying themselves. She spoke perfect French and would recite French poems delightfully. One evening she described to us a round of visits that she and her husband had paid to his ducal and princely relations in Germany. She described this older Germany inimitably, and her gift for mimicry, which would have carried her far on the stage, brought to life the interminable evenings of conversation round a large polished table, of a boredom hardly imaginable.

Sylvia in her extreme youth had been a Maid of Honour in the last year of Queen Victoria's life and then to Queen Alexandra. She was interested entirely in people, and collected and retailed gossip vividly. She died in the Second World War, having as a widow come to live in a small house on a village green near Henley. I passed near her house the other day and thought of her with a pang of sorrow. She was someone whom one continues always to miss.

Her husband, Edward Gleichen, painted small pictures. His sisters always said that he chose a comfortable spot, arranged his easel and paints, and then looked round to see what there was worthy of record by his pen and pencil. Sylvia did not write or paint, she recorded and interpreted life by her talk and her mimicry; her flair as a hostess for making people happy must still glow in some hearts that remember her.

Nina Cust—Mrs. Henry Cust—deserves to be recalled for many reasons, not least because I loved her. She was a part of my life, in my childhood, youth, middle age, until she died at the age of ninety. She was beautiful, not only by Edwardian standards; tall and slight with aquiline features and a piled up mass of dark hair which never varied in pattern through the years. Her husband, Harry Cust, editor of *The Pall Mall Gazette*, had had a brilliant start in life. He was slightly feared by his contemporaries; he could say devastatingly cruel things. Nina was a cousin of my mother, she was born Nina Welby, daughter of Sir William Welby and her mother was a Stuart Wortley. Victoria Lady Welby married a baronet in Lincolnshire and wrote philosophical books which were not very comprehensible to most of her relations and readers. When we were first married we went to see her at the house in Harrow where she had gone to live. She was hard at work with several secretaries, answering (she told us) the voluminous letters she received from America. She was kind to us, but showed none of the wistful sadness that old people are apt to show when young people take their leave. I was much impressed by her, she seemed so full of interest in all she was doing. "I should like to be like her when I am old," I remarked to my husband as we caught a local train back to London.

It is impossible to write of Nina without sadness. I remember her first when I was a child—a presence in a room which made few demands on any one. She had a kind of moonlit charm as she smiled slightly, like the moon coming out from behind a cloud. Children are immensely susceptible to beauty and mystery, and I was no exception. After I grew up and married I used to go to the Custs' lovely house in Delahaye Street in Westminster. (The whole street has now been swallowed up by government offices, I believe; a pity, because it was in an ancient *cul de sac*, an oasis in that part of London.) Nina's smile was less amused and more ironic as the harshness of life pressed more strictly upon her. Harry Cust had been, as I have said, editor of *The Pall Mall Gazette*, and to judge by what the people who worked with him said, a brilliant journalist. I only saw him in his later years, in his decline. We used to meet the Custs at Ashridge Park, the house of his uncle Lord Brownlow. Harry seemed lazy and lethargic, he was supposed to be writing a book on Machiavelli, but I don't think he ever finished it. As a husband he was unfaithful, cold and casual, but Nina loved him to the point of idolatry. She was very talented, a fine sculptress and she made a recumbent statue of Harry after his death (now in

XIII.   Mrs. Henry Cust

XIV.   Views of Piccadilly

Belton Church in Lincolnshire). My family loved and admired her and disliked Harry.

I remember lunching with him and Charles Whibley once when Nina was ill and I was alone with the two men. There was some sharp wit in the men's conversation but very little humanity. When I went upstairs to see Nina, she looked beautiful lying in bed surrounded by scarlet anemones some-one had sent her from the South of France, but always sad as from behind a cloud.

As well as being a sculptress, Nina was an admirable writer. Her highly erudite book about the Teutonic mediaeval knights, *Gentlemen Errant*, was much praised. In her extreme old age she put together an anthology called *The Tub of Gold Fishes*, the garnered sheaf of a lifetime's reading. Harry's nephew, Sir Ronald Storrs, says in his Preface to this book, "Here is an original anthology from the deep and wide, yet fastidious, 'casual' reading of a woman whose other known work, besides this little volume, are *Not all the Suns* and the grand sepulchral effigy in Belton church, which has long approved her mistress as well as devotee of the arts." Nina worked steadily and with concentration on her poetry and sculpture, but always left what she was doing at a moment's notice to serve Harry's slightest whim, and his whims were manifold and demanding.

After he died she went on living in their beautiful seven-teenth-century Chancellor's House in Hyde Park Gate. It was like a country house with lofty rooms, tree-shaded. Nina had arranged the rooms with a fine and distinguished taste, and the whole house was a hushed shrine for the recumbent statue of Harry Cust, a replica of the one at Belton. As the years went by I used to visit her there after deafness had come upon her and she received few people, but her interest in books and contemporary writing and other things of the mind never flagged.

I used, in the intervals of our talk, to look out of the tall window near her sofa at the Sleeping Beauty's garden outside, where a wild profusion of overgrown roses tapped on the window pane with a jungle of shrubs and trees beyond. It was an oasis in the grinding noise and bustle of London and a sad reminder of happier times. Nina never varied her long trailing dress; a large Edwardian garden hat lay on the chair beside her. Towards the end she drifted further away into the silence of impenetrable deafness. Chancellor's House and the marble statue of Harry Cust were to come under the house-breakers' hammer, but her "testament of never-ending love" endures:

". . . No wit of man may part us now or ever
Nor shall a mortal hand our dust dissever.
Under these strong square stones and shadowing eaves
Fast folded by our singing robe of leaves,
Hard by the old grey sun-washed, tree-walled tower,
We sleep in peace, awaiting God's great hour."

Marie Belloc Lowndes was a figure in literary circles in London when I was young, and a close friend of my mother's. She came to our house a great deal. She was short and round, and wore a charming Victorian bonnet which suited her very well. Her books contradicted the first cosy impression she made. Her best known, *The Lodger*, is about Jack the Ripper. She revelled in gruesome stories. She was extremely kind-hearted and the lurid tales which she so much enjoyed never affected her niceness and goodness to her friends. She was a welcome guest in many country houses and always an asset to any party, as she could be counted on to make dull people feel encouraged and happy. She was, surprisingly, a friend of Alexander Woollcott, the American writer and journalist—"an enchanting old woman who is a great crony of mine" he wrote of her during the War.

I always envied her (being a slow starter myself in the morning) because she rose at 6.30, made herself some tea and got on with her writing before her household began to stir and her multitudinous social engagements pressed in on her. How nice, I thought, to be so stalwart in the morning, especially after one had gone to bed late the night before.

In the Second World War Marie Belloc Lowndes always travelled with a large tin trunk in addition to a good deal of other luggage, in the days when most of us crammed our clothes in the smallest of small suitcases. This tin trunk carried a bulky apparatus for tea-making. Wartime railway stations were dimmed-out and bare of porters, but people were always very kind, she said, about helping her carry it—I am sure they were to her!

She lived in a small dark house in Westminster with her husband who was working on *The Times* and her two charming daughters. Her brother was Hilaire Belloc, and although she possessed none of his genius, she and he were exactly alike in their sturdy championship of everything French, at times when the needle of English public opinion spun round in an anti-French direction.

She has left one permanent addition to our literature in the haunting evocative story of her French childhood *I too Have Lived in Arcadia.*

Arthur Balfour* was a lifelong friend of my mother's family. He had been engaged to May Lyttelton who had died during their engagement, and in his eyes all Lytteltons were his kin. We were doubly related to the Lytteltons, firstly by a rather remote cousinship, and secondly by the fact that my aunt Katherine Stuart Wortley had married Neville Lyttelton —son of Lord Cobham.

Occasionally, as I grew up, I shook hands with him and his

---

* Born 1848. Died 1930. Prime Minister 1902–1905. Leader of the Opposition 1906–1911. Foreign Secretary 1916–1919.

sister, Alice Balfour, at parties. I heard him discussed, criticised and approved, but after my marriage I came to know him better as he made friends with my husband. He was supposed to be wickedly bored by aspiring young Conservatives, but although my husband was nursing the constituency of Peebles and Selkirk in the Conservative interest, Arthur Balfour discovered in him a kindred spirit—and we were invited sometimes to dinner in London and to go for a weekend to Whittingehame and to the family party given by the Edward Talbots (Edward Talbot was then Bishop of Rochester) which took place yearly on the anniversary of May Lyttelton's death. (Edward Talbot had married a Lyttelton, sister of the dead girl.)

My husband and Arthur Balfour no doubt started off by talking about politics, but my guess is that they reverted quickly to philosophy which they discussed with that ardour common to intellectual Scots. Invitations to Whittingehame were therefore gladly accepted.

It was said by some people that A.J.B. was born into the purple. This has always suggested to me shaded lights, luxurious bathrooms and exotic flowers. When we lunched at Carlton Gardens there were no flowers on the table, only small blue and white pots containing ferns. The rooms had the unselfconscious charm of fine furniture and interesting pictures lit by tall windows, but nothing that could be defined as luxury. Once my mother and I were shown Mr. Balfour's bedroom at Carlton Gardens; it seemed to me dark and bare. There was a sort of lectern by his bedside and on it a manual on bridge. My mother was amused by this but rather shocked, as she regarded card games not as an intellectual exercise, but as distraction for imbeciles. She put an exclamation mark or two on one of the pages. I don't know if A.J.B. ever saw them.

The bathrooms at Whittingehame were few and spartan.

The only touch of purple I could see was that beside each plate at breakfast stood a boiled egg, to be eaten or not as the guest would wish; and as there were many more interesting things to eat, it often remained firmly rooted in its egg-cup untouched. Accustomed as I was to a very frugal scale of housekeeping this struck me as extravagant.

I was put next to Arthur Balfour at some meals and he talked to me with kindly courtesy, but I found myself not talking as freely as I should have done if we had been alone. It was known that his family watched carefully to see how any guest was getting on with him, and commented about it afterwards. That had a quenching effect on me, for although I was accustomed to talking to clever men, from my father onwards, the sense of being observed and assessed by the Balfour family reduced me to tongue-tied silence and I fear dullness.

When A.J.B. was in his study we relaxed in the drawing-room. There was much charm in his Balfour sisters-in-law. Lady Frances, red-haired and combative, was sometimes brusque but often amusing. Our mutual friend Archibald Flemming, Minister of the St. Columba's Presbyterian Church in Pont Street, had an uneven friendship with her which flared up sometimes into a stern disagreement. He accused her of wanting to "run his church" (the words were his). Lady Betty on the other hand was all charm and kindness and intelligence, someone to whom one could talk happily and with whom I felt always at home. To be with the Balfours was to be in an atmosphere where religion and philosophy were assumed to be the most important things in life—an experience which I am glad to have had.

Looking back on my first visit to Rome it all seems enchanted. I can only recapture what I felt in some novels of the period. Like Isabel in Henry James's *The Portrait of a*

Lady I had always been fond of history and "here was history in the stones of the street and the atoms of the sunshine". Like her, I had an imagination that kindled at the mention of great deeds. Like her, I felt the touch of a vanished world.

My mother had friends there and we went to the British Embassy, which had been decorated with stout and indefinite cupids on ceilings and murals by an artistic ambassadress. We also visited *palazzi* filled with flowers and books and musical instruments. Here writers and artists talked on a rarefied intellectual plane, while tourists and the Roman populace went their way outside.

We drove in little horse-drawn carriages, and went to the Campagna for picnics, in which various Roman notables of ancient lineage took part. We heard the gossip which has circulated round Rome since it was built, and felt as if we were part of the ancient and romantic scene. We did endless sightseeing, and indeed the whole episode is like a fairy-tale, imagined but not real.

My second visit to Rome was not so enchanted. My mother took a small apartment on the Trinità di Monte. It was rather dark, but in the garden behind us were orange blossoms, whose scent was delicious. We had two Italian maids called by the charming names of Santa and Fride. My mother did a good deal of painting and I got to know Rome more thoroughly, and we were kindly entertained by various people. I am always glad we went to Rome a second time, though the rapture had faded of the first visit in my extreme youth. I am told it is now much changed. I like to think of it before the motor-car age as Henry James described it, nostalgically remembering the splash of the fountains and the flower stalls—and in the Campagna, now drained and utilised, "the far gradations and soft confusions of colour . . . the hills where the cloud shadows had the lightness of a blush".

A well-known figure in those days was Henry Brewster,

half American and half English, who lived in Rome and had no profession. He spoke several languages and seemed to me to be the fine flower of sophisticated cosmopolitanism. My sister and I named him the *Weltkind*. We had yearnings for that sort of cosmopolitanism ourselves.

In the days when leisure was founded on lavish domestic help and the power to converse pleasantly was a passport to the best society had to offer, men like Henry Brewster knew their own value. He was a type which, I imagine, the world will not see again, the product of a high civilisation, immortal for as long as Henry James's novels are read.

He had fair hair and a fair beard and his eyes were brown and wide apart. He had written several books of which *The Prison* (cast in the mould of a discussion on philosophy by three people) is, I believe, still read. In Ethel Smyth's Preface to it, she quotes from Maurice Baring's autobiography, *The Puppet Show of Memory*: "The most refreshing thing about Brewster was that he was altogether without that exaggerated reverence for culture in general and books in particular that sometimes hampers his countrymen (for he was an American), when they have been transplanted early into Europe and brought up in France, Italy, or England, and saturated with art and literature. He liked books, he enjoyed plays, poetry, and certain kinds of music; but he didn't think these things a matter of life and death. He enjoyed them as factors in life, an adjunct, an accompaniment, an interlude, just as he enjoyed a fine day. He liked people for what they were, not for what they had achieved."

We mostly saw him in company with Ethel Smyth, and a greater contrast could not be imagined than those two. Ethel was all force and fire, and was usually concerned in the production of an opera of which she had written the music. She wore what were called in those days "mannish" clothes, serviceable suits with short skirts and a cloth cap on her head.

A great friend of hers, Mrs. Crawshay, who was elegance itself, decided to ensure that when Ethel took a curtain call after one of her operas, she should be properly and suitably attired, and bought her a smart evening blouse with a matching long skirt. When the curtain rose Ethel Smyth was seen wearing the blouse, but alas, not the graceful black skirt, but one of her short workaday ones of thick useful tweed. Mary had also bought her a hat with bows of some magnitude on it. It was the custom in those days for milliners to stuff out the large bows on hats with tissue paper, when they sent them round to our houses. Ethel had not removed the paper and as she bowed it made a loud crackling sound.

I chiefly remember Ethel Smyth being thunderous at the piano. I once spent an evening when she played a Wagner opera from beginning to end, oblivious of the exhaustion of her listeners. Her mastery of the piano was magnificent, and it was an unforgettable performance and I was lucky to hear it.

Henry Brewster, silent and rather languid, seemed to be inhabiting a world of thought of his own, but that was the pose he chose to adopt. I quote a poem of his which has always pleased me:

> Je connais des gens qui travaillent
> J'en connais qui ont réussi
> Moi je ne ferai rien qui vaille,
> > Dieu Mèrci.
>
> Je sais que les siècles s'envolent
> Qui le jour d'aujourd'hui m'est doux
> Que j'ai l'âme lointaine et folle,
> > Et c'est tout.
>
> Un faucon là-haut se balance,
> Le vent se roule sur les près,
> Berce moi dans mon indolence,
> > Bois sacré.

Perhaps! Anyway it has a lovely cadence in it.

That Henry Brewster was not a complete idler his books remain to show. He and Ethel were like sunshine and thunder—but she was the greater of the two.

Many years later I was having tea one day with Virginia Woolf, when Ethel Smyth, limping and stone deaf, came into the room. In spite of her disabilities she dominated the conversation with some of her old vigour.

My mother had friends in the world of art, and one friendship which gave her special pleasure was that of Sir Hugh Lane.* He was a restless, highly strung man, seeming to my eyes unsure of himself. Wherever he went he provoked controversy. Of his great artistic achievements much has been written and said. He brought the Post-Impressionists into the rather faded world of conservative British art. Some people dismissed him as a picture dealer, others said he was an idealist—someone nicknamed him the "Idealerist". Nicknames are apt to be shallow, snapshot appraisals, but this one held a deeper truth than usual. Hugh Lane *was* a dealer (after all he had to live and to make money), but he was also an idealist who wanted to bludgeon people into seeing beauty where before they saw only oddity and strangeness. He had a persuasive tongue and cajoled sometimes reluctant people into being painted (or having their relations painted) by artists who he thought should be given work.

In Edwardian and late Victorian times visitors to the Royal Academy expected pictures to be anecdotal—two lovers standing on a bridge, someone reading a letter, or an episode from classical mythology about the meaning of which there could be no two opinions.

I have read somewhere that when a cargo of live cod is sent to this country from Scandinavia the fish are apt to get dull and inert and therefore tasteless for eating. A cat-fish is

* Born 1875, he was lost in the *Lusitania* in 1915.

put in to bustle them about, and to keep them on the move and generally to act as a stimulus. Hugh Lane had this cat-fish power, and the art world in which he was a pioneer of new forms and thought reacted to his stimulus.

In my earlier youth I admired Burne-Jones and all the earlier Pre-Raphaelites. I still do, though I now see his weaknesses. Burne-Jones, who had been a friend of my father, illustrated his letters with pen-and-ink sketches that have a lightness and humour lacking in his large paintings. But he had a sense of grouping and pattern which will, I am sure, make his work survive, in spite of the rather static and pallid looks of some of the people he portrayed.

We went to every exhibition, usually more than once to the Royal Academy where a few fine pictures were hung amongst a good deal of inferior stuff. Sargent was greatly admired, praised and misunderstood. He was in advance of his time in some ways, and shocked and startled people who were accustomed to a tepid approach to portrait painting. Sir John Millais' pictures were sure of admiration; they usually told a story and told it very well. His paintings had fine colours and a decisive roundness of treatment, appealing both to the eye and to the heart. As an Edwardian I have always loved and admired "The Vale of Rest", two nuns sitting at dusk with a sunset sky behind their coifed heads, for the stillness and serenity it has.

A frequent visitor to our house and a figure in Edwardian days was General Sir Francis Lloyd.* He was a devoted admirer of my mother and a figure out of an earlier world of dandies. His hair was dark and he had a black moustache which as he grew older was certainly dyed and brushed with Eau de Javel. He was tall and well set up with a slight, firm

* Born 1873, he joined the Grenadier Guards in 1894. He commanded the second, afterwards the first battalion. He was severely wounded in the South African War. He also fought in the Swahili expedition and received many medals, foreign and English.

figure. He wore copper bangles and a fine handkerchief edged with lace peeped out of his breast pocket. He once explained to me that one must have two handkerchiefs, "a blower and a shower". I was always famous for dropping my handkerchiefs all over the place (my husband put this characteristic foible of mine into one of his books—making the heroine who has been kidnapped traceable by a dropped handkerchief) and I was much impressed by this remark.

General Frankie, as he was called, belied his appearance completely. His dandyism was for its own sake. In conversation he was downright; he disliked what he called "nonsense", and in his view there was a great deal too much nonsense about in the world.

He once angrily told my mother that the father of one of his young relations refused to let his son take up a job in South Africa. My mother enquired why this was and General Frankie replied, "Why, just because of sin, and fiddle-de-dee!"

The Lloyd household was run on military lines. I remember their wonderful butler who had been General Frankie's batman, and one evening, when dinner was a fractional moment late, the General saying to him, "Go and give them perfect hell in the kitchen". *Autres temps!*

To the General's great disappointment he was not sent to the 1914 war, but commanded the London district. He was very severe about the far-fetched spy stories which are current at the beginning of any war. I rashly repeated to him some story of carrier pigeons being released by enemy agents, to which he replied, "Well, don't go gossiping and gabbling about it. Get the facts and then report it in the proper quarter." I stopped repeating spy stories after this.

The Lloyds' hospitality was lavish, they had innumerable servants, and their dinner table sparkled with silver. All the silver they possessed was crowded in a picturesque miscellany in front of us as we dined, teapots and all.

We went for expeditions with the Lloyds into Wales, dressing for dinner every evening in our most elaborate clothes and enjoying ourselves thoroughly in the manner of those days; and if there was nothing remarkable in the conversation of the guests it had left a pleasant memory in my mind of the Georgian house, their hospitable kindness and General Frankie's curt and sensible remarks which so remarkably contradicted his foppish exterior.

I HAD the good fortune to know intimately for some years a piece of Edwardian Scotland—the small town of Peebles and its surrounding countryside, also Selkirkshire.

Before I met my future husband, I had stayed with my mother in one or two country houses in Scotland, where much of the everyday life went on as it did in England. My hosts knew London well, and had intermarried with English families who were related to mine and I was therefore on recognisable ground.

The sport was different. There was endless fishing and rushing rivers, and there was often the sound of pipes in the air. But these visits had given me no inkling of what another part of Scottish life was like. My in-laws were completely Scottish and had not a drop of English or other blood in their veins. My husband in London and Oxford and my brother-in-law, Willie, in India had gone out into the world, but my parents-in-law had made only one journey to South Africa. Anna had climbed adventurously in Switzerland and had briefly visited London, and Walter had climbed with John in the Island of Skye. But my mother-in-law seemed to meet only Scottish people wherever she went, and she hugged her Scottishness to her like a garment. She had a deep distrust of anything English, thought bishops odd and absurd, and never scrupled to say sharp things about England. Her sons' careers at Oxford didn't interest her much, although she was pleased when they received university prizes. But she felt it to be only their due, nothing more.

I went up to Peebles when I was engaged to be married

and was plunged into a wholly unfamiliar life. We had prayers every evening and hymns were sung. I was a church-goer of the Anglican persuasion, but my parents were agnostics and I was unfamiliar with all this. It is true that at Moor Park we had had family prayers which all the servants attended in rows; but there were only a few prayers read and a psalm, and it took place after breakfast and was soon over. My father's much older sisters were absorbed in church matters and my grandfather, who was low church, did a good deal in church affairs, so I had a background of prayers and church-going. But this availed me nothing with my mother-in-law who acknowledged only one true church, her own branch of Presbyterianism. Being an Anglican, as I was, didn't really count for righteousness in her eyes.

In myself she was presented with a sort of portent; a girl who lived in the world of London and went to parties, who was English, and whose mother had servants to do her house-work, who belonged to another church. She fiercely disliked the idea of her children marrying, and that her beloved son John should make his life and work in London and marry a girl from there made her deeply unhappy and resentful. Anna, my sister-in-law, and I loved each other from the start (though she could be militantly Scotch). We had the same sense of humour and, even when no longer young, were often stricken by the oddities of life into explosive laughter together.

I remember one occasion at an afternoon party in a country house, where a minister, who we anyhow thought slightly absurd, recited "Gunga Din" with mournful emphasis. During the recitation, one of his waistcoat buttons caught the frond of a potted plant while he continued to thunder out Kipling's verses. For some reason this struck us as wildly funny and we disgraced ourselves with suppressed but audible giggles.

We held post-mortems on every tea party and every social which we attended, and mimicked people who sang or recited in a way we thought ridiculous. Anna's own recitations were beautifully done. She was a very talented actress and would have liked to have gone on the stage, but this was unheard-of in a minister's daughter of her generation. My future mother-in-law's talk was much of church matters, of Wee Frees and U.Ps; to me words quite incomprehensible, though John, with the greatest tact and patience, explained all this to me and helped me at every stage of the way on this difficult visit. The thing which charmed me and made me happy was the Buchans' love of books, and I found to my joy that we had exactly the same tastes in literature. They knew far more poetry by heart than I did, and it played a great part in their lives. Money was not plentiful but they seemed to have all the books that anyone could want. We went for some drives; one I remember to Hangingstow in Selkirkshire where an old bachelor cousin of the Buchans lived in a dark house with a garden which descended in terraces from the house. I duly admired the garden, but the house struck a chill to my spirit. I had visited dark and gloomy houses before, but they were never quite like this.

Peebles, in those days, was a little town with a High Street of little shops with friendly shopkeepers. Mrs. McGillivray, the greengrocer, who on being asked what fruit she had in that day, would answer cheerfully, "Nothing startling in the pear line." Mr. Veitch sold fishing tackle, and years afterwards his shop was to be the favourite haunt of my eldest son. At Mr. Goudburn's, the baker, every kind of delicious "tea bread", as it was called in Peebles, was to be found. Miss Smith of the sweetie shop sold her own home-made toffee and other sweets. Shopping in Peebles with Anna was a delight to me, accustomed as I was to the larger but much less intimate London shops.

The churches, of which there were several, were always packed, and one had to go early to find a seat. Sermons were eagerly discussed, and comparisons made between one minister and another. I found it hard at first to enjoy a service with extempore prayers which went on and on, and I missed the splendid ritual of the Anglican service; but I enjoyed the sermons, and later in my life became what was called in Scotland "a sermon-taster"—someone who would go to any church where the preaching was excellent. (I did this in London whenever I could.) I remained an Anglican, supported by my husband who saw no reason for me to change my church.

I was struck by the loveliness of Peeblesshire; it reminded me of happy times at Simonstone in Wensleydale, of my childhood and early youth. The fields with their stone dykes and the rounded hills have a likeness to their Yorkshire counterparts. Bank House, where the Buchans lived, next door to the Commercial Bank of Peebles, was cheerful, old with some nice old furniture, and books everywhere. Open house was kept at tea-time when my mother-in-law's home-baked scones and shortbread were famous, and visitors stayed long and were loth to leave. The Bank House circle was much enlarged when my husband began to nurse the constituency (then called Peebles and Selkirk) and we got to know people in the country houses as well as the smaller houses, farms and villages. But all this came later.

After my engagement visit I returned to London and went to stay, accompanied by my mother, with my aunt at Ockham Park. The air of Surrey, in a house surrounded by trees, seemed heavy and lifeless after the brisker air of the north, and life in a country house slow and dull after the vividness of the Buchan household and their keenness about everything. My mother-in-law's ferocious activity had impressed me forcibly and I admired her; and as our children came along and sorrows swept over us we became fast friends.

"You get on with Gran because you've got a sense of

humour and can see that she is funny," Anna once said to me.
Anna and I continued our loving relationship through two
wars and the years between until she died. Her last dying
words to me were: "We've had so much fun together, my
dear." She was that rare creature, a woman of deep piety and
goodness who could laugh even when sorrows crowded over
her, and whose generosity and love of giving was proverbial
to all those who knew her. Anna did not publish any books
until after Edwardian days, when she became a highly
successful and best-selling novelist, writing under the name
of O. Douglas. Her books should be read by all interested
in Glasgow and the Scottish Border countryside early in this
century. Her Glasgow novel, *The Setons*, has a great deal
of autobiography in it. It is about the life of a widowed
minister and his daughter, Elizabeth Seton, and a small son
living near a church in Pollokshields. The minister is a clear
picture of my father-in-law, an absent-minded and saintly
man; the daughter has much of Anna herself and the small
boy is her brother Alastair. The household is a happy one, full
of cheerfulness and comfort, poetry and books, though cash
is scarce. The sight, smells and vigorous activity of Glasgow
are very well portrayed. All her life Anna loved Glasgow
and its kindly, cheerful, hospitable people; but she was also
amused by some of their oddities and affectations.

She describes a small house where a party was to be given
by a Mr. and Mrs. Thomson: "On the left side of the door
as you entered was a large room with a bow window and two
side windows. . . . The wallpaper was yellow with a large
design of chrysanthemums, and the woodwork white without spot or blemish. The thick Axminster carpet of peacock
blue was covered with yellow roses. It stopped about two
feet from the wall all round, and the hiatus thus made was
covered with linoleum which rather unsuccessfully tried to
look like a parquet floor. There were many pictures on the

wall in bright gilt frames, varied by hand-painted plaques and enlarged photographs. The suite of furniture was covered in brocade in a shade known as "old gold", and a handsome cabinet with glass doors and shelves covered with pale blue plush held articles which had pleasant memories for the Thomsons; objects of art from the Rue de Rivoli (they had been to Paris for a short holiday) and cow bells and carved bears from Lucerne.

" 'There is nothing that enlarges the mind like travel,' was a favourite saying of Mr. Thomson and his wife who never failed to answer: 'That's true, Papa, I'm sure.'

"The piano stood open with *The Rosary* on the stand; the incandescent lights in their pink globes were already lit.

" 'Well, well,' said Mr. Thomson, 'you've been successful with your colour scheme, Mamma. I must say that the yellow and white's cheery and the blue of the carpet makes a fine contrast. You've taste right enough.' "

The party and all its humours is admirably described. There was grim poverty in Glasgow alongside riches and comfortable middle-class life, and Anna puts in some vivid and heart-rending pictures of the poverty of the people her heroine, Elizabeth, visits in the slum tenements. The Church played, of course, a very large part in the life of a minister's family, and the descriptions of their Sunday observances would stagger any churchgoer of today. They spent the whole of each Sunday in church at service after service, eating sandwiches and Bovril in the vestry in the middle of the day.

The book closes in the 1914 war and describes the young men going off and being reported killed and missing, and the repercussions on their families. Mr. Seton, whose faith in an after-life is completely sincere and fervent, has his work cut out to try to console the bereaved in the country parish to which he has retired.

I will not attempt to describe John's and my adventures as

a Conservative candidate and his wife. Anyone who has nursed a constituency knows the tale of hurried and unsuitable meals (which had a very bad effect on my husband's health), the cold and gloomy halls, the by-products of sociability. I helped John all I could, trying my hardest to understand the Border speech and, what was even more difficult, making our hoped-for constituents understand my English way of talking. I remember one nice stout farmer's wife leaning out from her chair and saying in a confidential tone, "Butter is an awful *vex*." I had some difficulty in making a suitable rejoinder. She obviously meant the making of butter, a commodity I had only seen neatly laid out on plates at tea-time—I knew nothing of the intricate process of making it. But somehow I managed to make friends. I think they knew goodwill and a striving for understanding when they saw it.

Peebles and Selkirk, too, were strongly Liberal in politics and I doubt if in those days my husband would have won the seat. (In the end he never stood for it.) The two mill-owning families, the Ballantines and the Thorburns, on different sides of politics dominated the scene in Peebles. I remember a bazaar got up to give a bowling green to the town. Anna and I had worked our hardest to gather a stall together and I had brought objects of all sorts from London. I knew someone in Edinburgh who had a hat shop, and persuaded her to send us some hats on sale or return as I thought they would be a novelty in Peebles. They arrived and we unpacked them with pleasure; they were neatly fitted to the head and had rather an austere smartness. But they did not sell well. My mother-in-law, with her devastating habit of crossing her "t"s and dotting the "i"s of every situation, remarked: "Hats with more *appearance* than these would have excited the Peebles people more."

She was right (she always, alas, was right), we should have had impressive hats with feathers and bunches of flowers on them.

All our hard work resulted in our making a good profit on the stall and the Ballantine stall fell well behind us in takings; but Sir Henry Ballantine, unwilling that the Conservatives should score a triumph, made up the takings of his wife's stall to exactly our figure out of his own pocket. Anna and I thought that not quite cricket; after all our hard work we should have been allowed a modest triumph.

The Scotland of those days lies behind me and has a sunlit place in my memory. I seem to recall so much happiness and fun and interest. When I had fitted myself into the life of Peeblesshire it became congenial and interesting. Going there was like going to another country, different from London and from all one did and said there, and always interesting in the strong individuality of its different points of view. There was always the excitement of some tale of Scottish achievement overseas, for the Scots are one of the most far-flung peoples of the world; and the contrast between this and the intimate social life of a little town, with its cosy living and round of church and business, was charming.

I remember how my mother-in-law would say with a sigh when she seated herself by a magnificent fire, in front of a heavy teapot and plates full of scones and shortbread: "Well, it's a grand thing—*comfort*."

Peebles now has supermarkets and the little shops have mostly gone. Bank House as a hospitable centre is no more. It is now filled with typewriters and bank clerks, and only remains in the memories of a few ageing or aged people. But, while it lasted, it stood for a place where the gay and frivolous and the aged and lonely were always welcomed and made to feel at home.

The shadows still chase each other across the surrounding hills, and a faint bleating can be heard from the many sheep which wander on their steep slopes; but the Peebles I knew has gone.

WHAT does it all add up to, when we look back at this curious Edwardian age, poised between Victorian times and two great wars?

It is called by some an age of glitter and squalor, a design of elegance and rags, or of brass and iron. These years are praised for their opulence and security on the one hand, and blamed for the background of poverty on the other. The Edwardian years have been misunderstood by those who have read the catchwords about them, and have never gone more deeply into the story of what really happened.

The Victorian era is much easier to grasp. We read of horse-drawn traffic, quiet country scenes, strongly held religious views and a rigorous moral code. We look at pictures of crinolines and poke bonnets, and we have been well instructed by historians on the facts of the Industrial Revolution. The Victorians are far enough away from us in time to be viewed in perspective. A far greater effort of imagination is needed to get a clear picture of the later age of which I have written and I (like those living people who are Edwardians) should show what it is like to have lived in those times.

The vision of people of today is obscured by the smoke and flames of two wars. We exist in a disillusioned and dis-illusioning time, and can only see as blameworthy the enviable complacence in which the Edwardians lived. Nevertheless, in the later years of King Edward's reign our rulers (and many thinking people) were deeply disturbed by the growing menace of Germany as shown in her expanding naval programme; but most British citizens went on with their lives, regardless of the fact that the dragon's teeth had been sewn in the fields of Europe, and would rise up one day as armed men.

Rainer Maria Rilke wrote in the 1914 war "after this war we shall have lost our innocence". He was right. In the harsh and insecure life in which we now live, bludgeoned by news from all quarters all the time, the milder writers of innocence and romantic imaginings have completely gone; and we have come to feel a kind of envy and suspicion about a happier past age.

Walter de la Mare sums up the 1920s in these words: "The very years that we now so actively occupy will soon be packed up in an old satchel . . . and our little hot, cold, violently affected, brand new, exquisite, fresh little habits of mind, manners, hobbies, fashions, ideals, will have thinned and vanished away, will steadily have evaporated, leaving only a frigid deposit of history, a few decaying buildings, some music, some machine-made voices, an immense quantity of print". . .

To the frigid deposit of Edwardian history I hope to have added my little touch of warmth, and to have told something about a time in which I lived with so much happiness, love, and friendship, and where I tasted the joys of a quieter and more uncrowded world.